THE AUTHOR : TONY YEP

1st Paperback Edition

A Collection of

THE STORIES MY FATHER TOLD

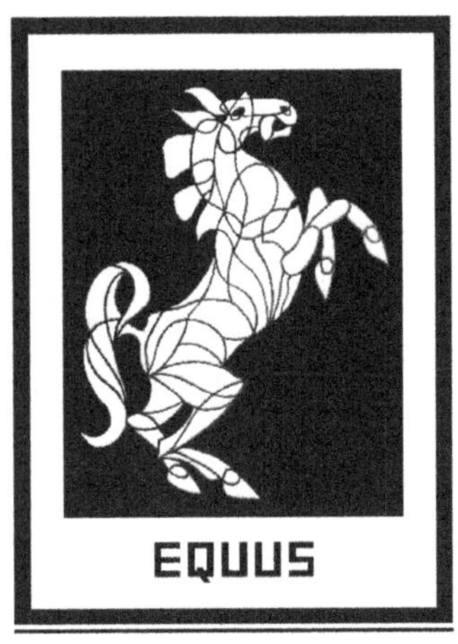

A STYLIZED STALLION
Depicting the
Uniqueness of the
Eclectic Stories
In this Book

A Collection of

THE STORIES MY FATHER TOLD

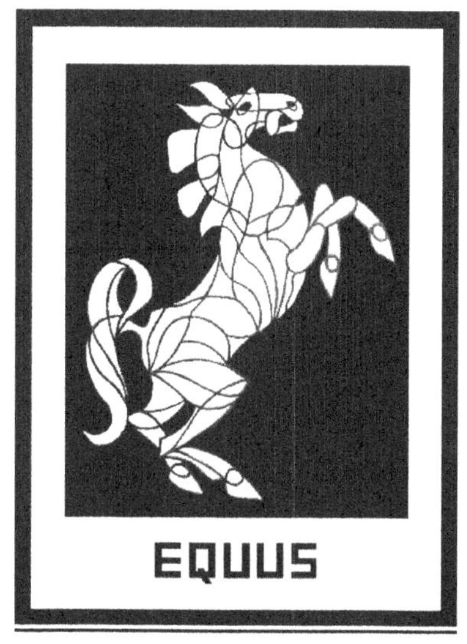

TONY YEP

<u>**DEDICATION**</u>

These stories about my life could not have been written without the involvement and support of my wife, Patricia. She has always been the love of my life.

ACKNOWLEDGEMENTS

I would like to acknowledge the following people who helped make my second book another "Once in a Lifetime" endeavour.

A very special thanks to **Mary O'Neill** who provided the editorial reviews and comments. Her invaluable insights made my stories worth reading.

Many thanks again to my brother-in-law, **Steve Roper** (www.steveroper.ca), who finalized the book cover layout.

Final acknowledgement and appreciation to my wife, **Patricia**, who has always been the best critic of my written works!

TABLE OF CONTENTS

FRONT TITLE PAGE i
"EQUUS" COVER DESIGN ii
MAIN TITLE PAGE iii
COPYRIGHT iv
DEDICATION v
ACKNOWLEDGEMENTS vi
TABLE OF CONTENTS vii
PREFACE xi

Chapter 1
HORS D'OEUVRES

1 - The First Story 1
2 - Carmen at the Sydney Opera House........... 3
3 - What Makes a Good Story?........................ 8
4 - Something About Mary............................. 13

Chapter 2
THE EARLY YEARS

5 - The YEP Family in Canada.......................... 17
6 - One Less Sister and Brother...................... 25
7 - Life in a Kite! 32
8 - Family Secrets 34
9 - The Things Chinese Eat! 44
10 – The Big Rat 48

11 – What Really Matters in Life........................ 50
12 - What My Father Never Told Me 53

Chapter 3
RESTAURANT STORIES

13 – Chinese Restaurants in Montreal 61
14 – There is No Plum in Plum Sauce 70
15 – A Lunch Working with Rita 76

Chapter 4
OF MEN AND WOMEN

16 – "Unrealistic Expectations"........................ 79
17 – First Impressions 82
18 – The Superiority of Women 90
19 – Middle of the Way 94
20 – Yin and Yang 96
21 – Oxymoron – Thinking Outside the Box! 99
22 – Judge Judy 102
23 – On Compatibility..................................... 106
24 – "Ando and Dating" 112

Chapter 5
MY GREAT KOREAN ADVENTURE
<u>Story 25</u>

– The Beginning 115
– The Geriatric Gang 118
– The Engineering Differences 120
– Challenging Said 123
– Electrifying Sharana 125
– Work at SK Tower 127

– Life in Seoul 129
– The Wives in Seoul 132
– Dining with the Locals 135
– The Alluring Ladies of Seoul 138
– The Ending 141

Chapter 6
IN SEARCH OF ALEXANDRITE
Story 26
– How It All Started 145
– Essentials of Gemstone Collecting 150
– What is Alexandrite? 155
– Finding Alexandrite 158
– The Appraisal 165
– An Excellent Outcome 170

Chapter 7
POTPOURRI
27 – Group of Seven Nudes! 173
28 – What Inhibitions? 177
29 – Adventures on Nude Beaches 180
30 – Amethyst Hunting in Seoul 186
31 – Peking Duck 193
32 – Do You Believe in Fate? 199
33 – A Soulmate for Our Son 204
34 – Movies Worth Remembering 214
35 – Forays into the World of Auctions 219
36 – Hopelessly in Love 225

Chapter 8
ENGINEERING STORIES

37 – "Elephant in the Grass!" 227

38 – On Being Lucky 231

39 – Dumb Things Engineers Do! 233

40 – Anyone Can Do Engineering! 240

41 – It's a Man-Made World 249

42 – Standing Behind Your Work 252

43 – A Million Dollars Bonus – Not! 265

Chapter 9
LIFE IN RETIREMENT

Story 44   273

– Rule #1 - Confirm Mate for Life 275

– Rule #2 – Establish Support 277

– Rule #3 – Work and Retirement Plan 278

– Rule #4 – Take Care of Yourself 279

– Appendix (10 Sections) 281

Chapter 10
THE LAST STORY

45 – What's in a Name? 289

RECOMMENDED READING 293

ABOUT THE AUTHOR 295

PREFACE

Has your father ever told you stories about his life adventures? Stories that were so interesting and unique that you were held spellbound, waiting to hear what came next. My father did tell many such stories and he was a great story teller. He had the natural knack of making his stories so captivating no matter what the subject matter was. Unfortunately, all my father's stories had been verbal and he never recorded any of them in writing. These are the memories I hold dear to me and I did not want to forget his engaging tales. I wrote this book to capture some of his best stories so they would not be forgotten. As I am also a father and a grandfather, I have included many of my own stories to carry on his tradition of story-telling.

I remember the first time I saw the movie "Forrest Gump." It deservedly won the Best Picture Oscar in 1994. The storyline was very strange, yet totally compelling, with interesting characters that were real and comforting. I sat in the theatre completely engrossed with the movie as the scenes unfolded. I had no idea where the movie was taking me and how it would end, but it was a thoroughly enjoyable journey of discovery. I wrote my book along this line keeping the topics of my stories fairly diverse and very eclectic. For many years I had been writing short stories which were included in my yearly newsletters. I never knew what the topic I would write about, but it was generally about my experiences and what life meant to me. Often, it was about my relationship with my wife, Pat, or with family and friends. Sometimes, it was about work or travel. Almost always, it included my general observations of people and the interesting and unusual things they did.

So, find a comfortable chair, relax and select a story that you might find interesting. Let me share with you my stories in the best tradition of "The Stories My Father Told."

Chapter 1

HORS D'OEUVRES

<u>Story #1</u>

THE FIRST STORY

This was the first story my father, Albert, told me. I will always remember his first impression of Canada. According to the Cantonese who first immigrated to Canada, Canada was called "Gam San," literally translated, Golden Mountain, to reflect a land of plenty and riches. The Yep family first settled in Chinatown in downtown Montreal. Every week, the local Canadian butcher nearby would throw out garbage cans filled to the brim with oxtail and chicken claws. Oxtail was not valued back in those days and nobody ever ate the chicken claws which were essentially seen as inedible "crap".

My father would take all these goodies back home and the very large Yep clan would feast royally every week and for free! In particular, the chicken claws were considered to be a delicacy in China and they never had so much given to them for nothing. For him, Canada was such a great country and the Canadians were so rich that they thought nothing about throwing away such delicacies! I asked him why the chicken claws were so valued. Bemused by my ignorance, he said the chicken claws were the best part of the chicken because they were simply delicious! He asked whether I knew how many chickens you had to kill to get so many claws? He said that one chicken has only two claws, and in China, it was not practical to slaughter so many chickens just to get enough claws to make a decent meal.

Keep in mind that chicken claws are just skin and bones and you have to strip off the scaly outer membrane to make them edible. They are sought after because they are indeed very tasty. If you have ever gone to a Chinese dim sum and tasted the braised chicken feet with black bean sauce (fung chow), then you will know what I am describing. But like anything that can be eaten, you have to get past the look of what you are eating! Be adventurous. You might even like what you eat! Then you might not! That's life.

<u>Story #2</u>

CARMEN AT THE SYDNEY OPERA HOUSE

W hen my wife and I first visited Sydney, Australia in 2002, we saw one of its most iconic landmark, the striking Sydney Opera House. Wouldn't it be nice to actually see an opera there? As luck would have it while we were there, they were playing the opera, Carmen. You know the classic story of Carmen, that provocative, lithe and beautifully seductive gypsy woman who uses her feminine guile and alluring beauty to seduce and captivate the handsome, but hopelessly trapped, Don Jose.

This was my ideal of what a beguiling woman should be with the beauty and sex appeal that would make men fall helplessly under her spell and do her every bidding. Accompanied by the dynamic music of Georges Bizet, it was one of the best and most popular opera. All this was good, and the appearance of the leading lady singing the Carmen role appeared attractive enough. When we got to our hotel in Sydney, I asked the concierge to try to get some tickets to the opera. Only 1st balcony seats were available, and I still had to pay a high price of over $150 for each ticket! I was hesitant at first as I had never paid such an exorbitant amount for any show or concert! But then it was the one-and-only Carmen, the most famous opera, being played at the renowned Sydney Opera House. What could be any better? At that price, it had to be good! How many people could claim to have experienced such a once-in-a-lifetime event? I talked myself into it, bit the bullet and bought the tickets.

Now the Sydney Opera House is known world-wide for its dramatic architectural design. What we didn't realize was that its iconic sail-like roof structure was made up entirely of blue mosaic tiles. We also found out that the original design by the Danish architect, Jorn Utzon, was not followed. Instead of one large main theatre, four smaller ones were built. That explained why the ticket prices had to be so costly. In the smaller venue, they still needed to cover the high production costs of Carmen with its many cast members, costumes, stage settings and the live orchestral music. But the smaller theatre was very intimate with wonderful acoustics. We could see and hear everything very clearly from our seats.

On the day of the opera, I found out that the lead singer advertised in their brochures was not playing Carmen that night for some personal reasons. Her understudy was doing the role of Carmen. This was usually not a good thing as the understudy would rarely surpass the leading star. But we were committed to going and I was looking forward to the opera. Now before I proceed further, I must offer my apologies to all my readers who might consider themselves to be "spatially challenged." Is this the politically correct way of saying pleasingly plump?

The opera started fine, the music was strong and familiar, the supporting cast members were energetic and engaging. The women milling about were young, good looking and sexy as expected. Then Carmen came out. Usually, when the star comes out, you could tell right away. My vision of Carmen was utterly shattered. Instead of a beautiful, sleek, sexually wanton and gracefully wild Carmen (yes, I always had an awesome imagination and very high expectations) in the classic "femme fatale" mode, I witnessed this generously proportioned woman who looked like and exuded as much sex appeal as Broom Hilda. I may be dating myself if I ask whether you know that big Viking wife who could sing opera in the comic strip Hagar! Then Don Jose came out …. you know, that tall, handsome and powerfully masculine soldier who will become utterly captivated by the seductive charms of Carmen. I asked myself, "Why are opera singers so short, big and beefy??!"

The famous seduction scene between Carmen and Don Jose was, to say the least, exquisitely painful to watch. They could both sing marvellously well, hitting all the high notes with power and passion. But I couldn't bear the sight of Carmen. She was purposely dressed in black to make her look slimmer and she wore a lot of make-up on her face to make her appear younger. She tried unsuccessfully to dance provocatively before a short and squat Don Jose who in his red uniform, looked every bit like a fire hydrant. I wanted to close my eyes and look away, but I couldn't. It was so fascinating in a perverse sort of way. It reminded me of those dancing hippos in ballet tutus in the Disney film Fantasia. While the music was great and the singing superb, the images were so discordant!

I guess good opera singers need to have some girth or size to be able to sing well. I remember seeing the Phantom of the Opera in Toronto a year later, and the woman playing the lead role of Christine was really beautiful and slim too. But she couldn't sing well nor hit the high notes especially in her signature song. It was embarrassing to hear her singing, trying but failing. Which is better - someone who can sing, but doesn't look the part, or looking the part, but can't sing? Neither works. I will always remember the Sydney Opera House, but maybe for the wrong reasons. The image of big Carmen dancing will forever be permanently etched in my mind! It was a good thing that I was going to see the ballet version of Carmen later on that year. Nothing like a good-looking prima ballerina and the other slim and athletic ballet dancers in tight fitting costumes leaping effortlessly about the stage to restore my image of the seductive Carmen.

And my wife thought I went to the ballet for culture!

Story #3

WHAT MAKES A GOOD STORY?

Everyone has an interesting story – something they did or happened in their lives that others might not have ever done or experienced. It's just a matter of how the story is told. My father had this innate knack of telling wonderful stories from the simplest events that most people could relate to. My son, Tim, once told me about the testing procedures that medical students were subjected to before they became doctors. He described in a ho-hum fashion how the student doctors were tested as if such events were quite normal and not that interesting. Maybe they were to doctors, but I saw a topic in his story that sometimes things in life happen because it was meant to be. Here is my version of his story.

In his final year of medical school, one of these tests involved the doctor's ability to do accurate diagnosis of various ailments by physically examining and questioning real patients. Doctors were really like detectives trying to find out what was really wrong with the people coming in to see them. They would ask their patients what was ailing them, to describe their symptoms, and then checking them out physically for obvious clues. They would get additional blood and other testing to search for other deficiencies. Then they would arrive at the most likely solution and cure to fix the problem. Even the dosage of medication prescribed would be a guess as everyone reacted differently to medication and their potential side effects. They would try something to see how it worked and then optimize the level or type of medication prescribed.

In this test scenario, ordinary people were hired as actors and they were given a list of ailments that would be described to the student doctors for them to figure out what was wrong. There were many such "actors" mimicking the symptoms of the various diseases they were to represent. There was a beautiful and buxom blonde in this group of actors. I guess she was selected as a distraction to the male medical students to see how well they would concentrate on their tasks at hand. At each station, a supervising or testing doctor watched the way the student doctors questioned and examined the patient, checking for their thoroughness in asking the right questions and the bedside manners and for professionalism between doctors and patients during the examination process. The assigned ailment for this young lady was carpel tunnel syndrome with the sharp pain from her elbow being felt into her chest area near her heart. All these actors were dressed in these terrible blue gowns with the open backs which made it very easy for the student doctors to perform whatever physical examinations were needed.

The young lady was sitting on the bed and she was greeted by the student doctor. "How are you today and what seems to be the problem?' he asked.

"My right elbow hurts when I bend it and my fingers and hand feel kind of stiff and numb. I also have some sharp pains moving about in my chest area." she said.

The student doctor immediately resisted in telling her the classic joke when a patient asks the doctor "Why does it hurts when I do this?" The answer being, "Well, just don't do that!" Obviously, having the function of her right arm was very important to the young lady. He suspected carpel tunnel syndrome and he made the young lady go through a range of arm, hand and finger motions asking questions what movements caused her pain or discomfort. The young lady was coached well to present all the right symptoms of her ailment. As she was also complaining about pain in her chest area, he had to check her heart to determine that the pain there was caused by her elbow and not the other way around.

He removed the top of her gown and started to listen to her heart moving his stethoscope to various positions from front to back. He also checked her body for skin abnormalities that might be causing the pain. But he kept going back to the heart, listening very intently. He seemed to be spending an inordinate amount of time probing and touching around her buxom area and the young lady was feeling a bit uncomfortable being exposed half naked all this time. She was getting impatient when she blurted out to the doctor, "It's my elbow! There is nothing wrong with my heart!" The student doctor, realizing that he spent too much time listening to her heart, told her that she was right. He concluded the examination and wrote on his test sheet the correct diagnosis of carpel tunnel syndrome.

Meanwhile, the testing doctor was observing all this with interest. He asked the student doctor on his way out to the other test stations why he spent so much time listening to this young lady's heart. "I thought I heard something," he said, "but it didn't have anything to do with her elbow." Now the supervising doctor was intrigued and he asked the young lady whether he could listen to her heart as well. He told her that the student doctor heard something in her heart, and that was why he had spent so much time keeping her exposed half naked all that time. He listened to her heart and sure enough, he heard something too. It was a faint "whooshing" sound and an almost inaudible irregular heart beat. He asked the young lady, "Did you have a congenital heart murmur when you were young?" "Yes," she replied, "but it never bothered me and I am perfectly fine and healthy." The doctor just nodded in agreement.

Well, it turned out that this supervising doctor was also a heart surgeon. Out of the hundred medical student candidates who took this test and examined this young lady, only this one young doctor heard this irregularity in the woman's heartbeat. He had a very remarkable skill in being so perceptive amongst his peers. As a result, this young doctor was highly recommended by the testing doctor to become a heart surgeon which he eventually became. Fate had intervened and it was meant to be. I have wondered ever since whether this young doctor ever married this beautiful young lady who ultimately determined the fate of his career as a doctor. Now that would be a fitting way to end this story! And it is all true! We have all met someone or did something that influenced and affected our lives in how we developed as a person.

Story #4

SOMETHING ABOUT MARY

I will always remember that period of time when Mary decided to run for School Trustee for the Catholic School Board which was the public school system in St. Albert. I was honoured that she trusted me as a friend to be her first campaign manager. We were young back then, full of hope and idealism – innocents in reality. We knew nothing of politics or what was really needed to get elected. We just wanted to do something which we believed would make a difference in our world. What would be more rewarding and meaningful than getting involved with the education of our children. We were living then in St. Albert, a small and vibrant city of 25,000 people just north of Edmonton. Her daughter and my younger son were in the same class and we got to know each other through our mutual involvement with the school and parent councils.

Yes, I was a neophyte manager with zero experience in running an election campaign. At that time, I was just an engineer who was taking some management courses in the evening at the university as I wanted to move up the corporate ladder at my workplace. Who knew then that my organizational skills would develop to be one of my greatest assets! One of the courses which I really enjoyed and had completed was marketing. So, I felt that I had some skills!? What an ideal opportunity to apply all the theories such as market differentiation, segmentation and advertising on a real-life situation! I was grateful that Mary believed in me and the strategies which we pursued.

I told Mary that her name was a very marketable name, strong and easy to remember and to recognize. Thanks to Jack's O'Neill family name and his Irish heritage! Mary already had a peerless reputation from her volunteer work as being a strong supporter of the school system and as someone with integrity and solid family and religious values. More importantly, she was a nice person you could trust! I had always admired Mary's skills in the way she interacted with people. You always felt comfortable around Mary and she made everyone feel like they were somebody important! People liked being in her presence. In hindsight, she made my first and only attempt as a campaign manager very easy and she was probably the main reason why I succeeded!

We did many things that were a first at that time. We were like mavericks trying to break through the old system of electioneering. We really didn't know if any of our new ideas would work. To differentiate ourselves from the rest of the candidates, we introduced the two-sided glossy 4" by 8" sized bio-cards printed on stiff cardboard instead of the standard photo-copied paper sheets. We won the "battle of the signs" by creating three custom-cut, hand-crafted and very large 4 ft. by 8 ft. wooden signs with her stylized name painted royal blue. They were uniquely different and eye-catching. They dwarfed all those other small signs used by the competition. These signs were so heavy and large, Mary had to get a couple of strong volunteers who owned a pick-up truck to move them about and strategically place them for maximum exposure on the main boulevards in the community. The campaign budget was limited to a modest $1000 which was essentially Jack's money. Other candidates would have greater sums of money to spend on their campaigns, having solicited donations from their supporters. Mary didn't want to rely on others for money and she didn't want to be obligated to anyone for doing something she strongly believed in. The bulk of this money was quickly used up by the signs and the bio-cards. We had to target the market by focussing our efforts solely on the Catholic School supporters as we only had a limited supply of bio-cards. Mary had many volunteers helping her as a lot of people liked her and they wanted to be part of her team. We got both the message and the voters out!

Our organization team was enthusiastic and the spirit was positive and wonderful! The whole campaign was actually a lot of fun! Losing was never in our minds, and we expected to win one of the vacant seats. What we didn't expect was to get the most votes. We even beat out the returning incumbents which was unheard of! Well, maybe in my initial naivete, I did. Remember that we were young then and we didn't know any better! To celebrate this momentous win, I made a specially glazed plaque which I gave to Mary. It had the number "2462" cut out of wood. This was the number of the people who believed in her and voted for her!

From this simple event, this started Mary's political career. In her continued commitment to public service, she got elected as a Member of the Legislative Assembly (MLA) for the province of Alberta. She was also a Member of the Senate and Board of Governors at the University of Alberta. If you are a believer of Fate, then you could say that "the Universe had unfolded exactly as it did" for Mary, because it was meant to be! These fond memories would last a lifetime for me!

Chapter 2

THE EARLY YEARS

THE YEP FAMILY IN CANADA

My great-grandfather, Charlie, was born in 1866 at the Pai Gee village of Sun Wui in the Guangdong Province in southern China. In 1892, he decided to come to Canada, arriving by boat in Victoria, B.C. Life in rural China was very harsh and there was much poverty. He would risk leaving his family, wife and son to travel to a foreign country half way across the world to seek fortune in the gold fields of British Columbia. All this just to get a better life for his family. Canada, known as Gam San or "Golden Mountain," was seen to be a prosperous land of riches with many opportunities for a good life. To build a national railway across its vast lands, Canada needed a source of cheap labour they found in the immigrant workers from China. Canada could not fulfill its national dream in building its country into a nation without the Chinese. He got his name "Charlie" when he first entered Canada. The immigration officer must have had difficulties in saying or spelling his "Duk Yee" Chinese name, so he just wrote down "Charlie." It must have been popular then to call any Chinese Charlies, but it is somewhat derogatory today as nobody is purposely called Charlie instead of Charles. Nevertheless, he ended up with this unusual English name.

At the turn of the century in 1900, it was a very difficult and lonely life for the Chinese men working and living alone without their wives or families in Canada. There was a lot of discrimination in those days. The Chinese could not speak the language, they looked strange and dressed oddly. They had no rights and they were not allowed to work as professionals or to own land. They were shunned by the general populace. There was no place for them to fit in. They were only tolerated primarily to provide cheap labour, doing the many low-paying menial and laborious work the Caucasians did not care nor wanted to do. As a result, the Chinese would end up going into either the laundry or restaurant businesses as these were the only work occupations open to them. I am forever grateful that when my ancestors immigrated to Canada over a hundred years ago, they chose to go into the restaurant business instead of laundry!

The Canadian population was mostly Caucasian and they simply didn't accept the Chinese as equals. They insisted on restricting their numbers to limit any negative effects on their society. This was reflected in 1882 by the Canadian Prime Minister, John A. Macdonald, who said that: "the Chinese were an alien race in every sense that would not and could not be expected to assimilate with our Aryan population." The Chinese Immigration Act of 1885 initially levied a head tax of $50 on every Chinese entering Canada. By 1903, this head tax was raised to an exorbitant $500! This was equivalent to over $15,000 in today's 2021 dollars - quite an obscene tax which applied only to Chinese immigrants giving them the "right" to provide cheap labour to Canada. How absurd! Further discrimination and hardships followed when this same Chinese Immigration Act was amended in 1923 to become an exclusion act, preventing almost all new Chinese from entering Canada. This lasted for 24 long years until it was repealed in 1947. The history of the Chinese in Canada included such overt discrimination by the Canadian government.

Like all Chinese, Charlie started out west, first in Victoria, then to Vancouver and he gradually moved east across Canada, following the Canadian Pacific Railway they had helped build. Some Chinese settled in the towns along the way, working in laundries or restaurants, or doing whatever work they could find and continued moving on. Charlie ended up settling in Montreal in 1899 where he found work initially as a launderer. He did very well as a laundryman to be able to afford a second wife! In 1902, he married a nice girl from the Lau family who lived in Vancouver. They had immigrated from China six years earlier. Charlie started a separate family in Canada, first with his second son, Eddy, followed by three daughters. Unfortunately, the Yep lineage ended with Eddy's family as he had five daughters and no sons to carry on the Yep name.

By the late 1910s, Charlie had changed professions. He became a successful merchant and manager of the Wah & Lung Dry Goods Company. In 1919 when his first wife died in China, Charlie brought his eldest son, Gwan Leung (my grandfather), who was already 27 years old, to Canada. My grandfather must have encountered another immigration officer who also had problems registering his Chinese name. This person must have had a warped sense of humour. Maybe seeing that his father was named Charlie, then why not name his son "Willie?" They seemed to be perfectly reasonable names for the father and his son! Willie had to work a few years to pay off the head tax of $500 and to save enough money to get his wife, Gam Bo (nee Young, my grandmother), and their four-year old son, Frank, to Canada in 1921. The following year, Charlie's twin grandsons, Albert and Alfred, were born in Joliette, Quebec. They were not only Canadian, but native Quebecois as well! Yes, Joliette, that very small town just 50 km northeast of Montreal. I have often wondered how my grandfather ended up there before finally settling in Montreal.

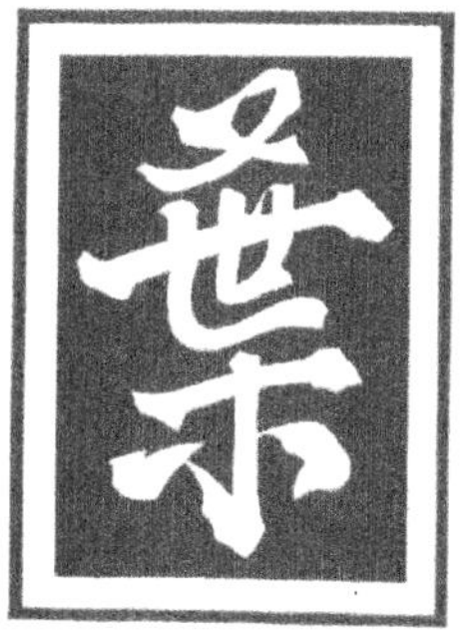

The Yep surname is a fairly obscure family name.
This YEP Chinese character literally means "leaf", like the leaf or leaves of a tree. There are few families of Yep origin in Canada.

It was not surprising that "Chinatowns" came to existence. There were no other places the Chinese could live and socialize. Chinatowns were essentially a "Bachelors Society" as they were mostly filled with single Chinese men. These men were separated from their wives and they supported their families who were still living in China. Occasionally, they took the long trans-Pacific journeys by boat back to China to visit and to have more children to carry on the family line. But they were the bread-winners and they had to return to their solitary existence in Canada.

The Chinese were well known for their love for gambling as what else was there for them to do? They created the Anglo-Chinese Social Club in 1936 for some diversions and to possibly include Anglo-Caucasians to be socially acceptable. Socializing even today meant gambling, and the Anglo-Chinese Club at 50 Lagauchetiere in Montreal was located right under the Nanking Restaurant at the corner of Clark St. Despite its very legitimate sounding name, this was the infamous "gambling joint" which Charlie was reputed to have started and owned. It was taken over later on by his son, Willie. I remember as a child of four or five years old to be taken there by my grandfather. He liked to show off his first grandson and he always let me play with the money in his caged off office area. Gamblers would drop by at the open wicket and pinched my cheeks because I was such a chubby kid, calling me "fey chai" meaning "fat boy" which I disliked! Being chubby back then was considered to be a good thing as this meant that the family was well off. My ancestors were definitely involved with gambling, whether legal or not. Charlie must have been rich judging by the professional studio portrait photos taken of the family members dressed in immaculate suits and expensive clothing. It was said that he owned four houses including one in the prestigious Town of Mount Royal where all the rich Caucasians lived!

It must have been very difficult for any Chinese to learn to speak English at that time, let alone learning to read and write the language. There were no formal government funded educational programs available then like we have today in Canada where new immigrants are encouraged and supported to learn English as their second language. It took Charlie much will power, perseverance and intelligence to learn multiple languages. It was said that he could even speak French after having multiple French girlfriends. He served as a translator/interpreter and advisor for the whole Chinese community. He was also involved with the Chinese Free Masons Association which was headquartered at 116 Lagauchetiere from 1928-1944. This place was located right next to the old Chinese Hospital and it eventually became my grandfather's house in 1949. All the Yep Family immigrated to Canada after the communist government in China took over power and confiscated the properties and lands from all the landowners after the Second World War. There was no intention of ever going back to China. Charlie was the first Yep in Canada, Yep #1, and his legacy was lasting.

Charlie Duk Yee Yep died in 1946. It was said that his funeral was a grand procession with well over 20 cars just to carry the flowers! He must had been an important person having the respect and friendship from people from all walks of life. His funeral was attended by many people, community leaders, politicians and dignitaries including the mayor of Montreal. This man had the most interesting and successful life of any of the Yep descendants. His life story was filled with intrigue, mystery and wonder. Railway worker? Laundry worker? Restauranteur? Grocery store merchant? Entrepreneur? Translator? Collaborator? Community leader? Casino owner? Gambler? Godfather? Who would ever know for sure?

Charlie was survived by his sons, Willie and Eddy. Willie and his wife had five sons and three daughters – Frank, Albert, Alfred, May, James, Gladys, Helen and Richard in that order. This became the genesis of the Yep family that exists today and continues to thrive in Canada.

Story #6

ONE LESS SISTER AND BROTHER

My father once told me that "When it is time for you to go, then it is time for you to go." Have you ever wondered how you have managed to live so long despite all the foolish and reckless things you may have done to jeopardize your own life and the lives of those around you? I remember a few incidents that could have drastically altered the course of my life, spinning it into an alternate reality I wouldn't have wanted. I could have had one less sister and one less brother because of my actions. But I was young then and I didn't know any better.

There was an event I recalled that happened when I was three or four years old. Normally, I shouldn't be able to remember things that happened when I was so young, but I did remember being under water. My older sister, Molly, and I were at the beach and we were sitting waist deep in the water along the shallow shoreline. For some reason, I fell backwards into the water and I couldn't get up. I just laid there submerged as the water covered my head. I vaguely remembered that my eyes were open looking up to the bright sky hazily shimmering through the water. My mouth was also open with water rushing in. Good thing my sister was looking after me and she sitting right next to me as I disappeared under the water. She saw this kid with his eyes open trying to swallow all the water on the beach. "Stupid brother!" she said, "You are supposed to keep your mouth closed!" as she pulled me up. That had always been my problem in keeping my mouth closed, even as I was growing up. I might have drowned that day if my sister had not been there. Children, when unsupervised, had been known to drown in less than a foot of water in their plastic wading pools in their backyards. It wasn't my time to go.

When I was six years old, the family was living at my grandfather's house. This was a ubiquitous three-story building with a flat roof, located in the heart of Chinatown in Montreal. For some reason, I thought it would be fun to go up to the roof to see what was there. I had never ventured up there, but there was a wooden ladder up on the third-floor balcony that provided access to the roof. I recalled taking my four-year old sister, Dolly, up with me as she was very adventurous and fearless. We never told our mother or grandmother that we were going to climb this ladder to the roof. We just disappeared and did this. It was a new adventure for us! When we got on the roof, being the older brother, I knew that there was an element of danger and that we shouldn't get too close to the edge. I was cautious and I kept low staying behind the 8" high parapet ledge that surrounded the roof perimeter. As I looked down, I could see that we were three stories high and it was a sheer 30 ft. drop to the concrete sidewalk and street below. No one told Dolly to be careful. Before I could say anything to her, she walked right up to the edge and stood on top of the parapet edge! I yelled at her, "Get back! Get off the ledge!" She just stood there with her arms spread out as if to say "Look at me! Look at me!" Obviously, she had no fear of falling or any vertigo looking down.

Strangely, my sister today has vertigo and is somewhat fearful of heights. But you wouldn't have known this when she was young. I breathed a sigh of relief when she stepped down back to the safety of the roof. I shudder when I think what would have happened if she did fall off the roof. It would have been all my fault for taking her up there and I would have been guilt-ridden for the rest of my life as would be my mother and grandmother who were supposed to look after their young children. Our lives would have been so negatively impacted. Good thing it was not meant to be.

Dolly said that this wasn't the only time I tried to "kill" her. She remembered the time when she was seven years old and I was trying to teach her how to swim. We were on a dock that jutted out into the water that was about six feet deep. Everyone was jumping off this dock and swimming about. My sister disliked the water because she didn't know how to swim. Again, being her older and presumably protective brother, I said, "What's the problem? Swimming is easy!" as I picked her up and threw her into the deep end. I firmly believed in the tried and true "sink or swim" method. Normally, people have a natural buoyancy which will make them float on top of the water. However, if you were fearful of water, your body would tense up and it would become denser. My sister sank like a rock to the bottom. As she was sitting on the bottom and holding her breath, she was thinking "When is my brother coming down to get me?" Meanwhile, I was waiting patiently for her to float back up, asking myself, "What was she doing on the bottom?" When it appeared that she wasn't coming up, I dove down and pulled her up to the surface. So much for the swimming lesson. Ironically, Dolly did learn how to swim, but not from me. She still couldn't swim very well, but at least she was no longer afraid to be around water. She even learned how to scuba dive so she didn't need to hold her breath while submerged! After these two incidents, that was it. If there ever was a third attempt, there would be no doubt that I would have one less sister!

I also could have lost my younger brother, Andy, who was four years old at that time and I was eight. Good thing he didn't remember this incident, but I did. In

Montreal, there was a big hill on St. Laurent St. running north to south from the busy Sherbrooke St. down to Ontario Street. St. Laurent was the main central street which divided Montreal from west to east. Wouldn't it be great to coast down the sidewalk on this street? It would be so much fun. So, I decided to share this adventure with my brother. My mother, having her hands full looking after five young kids, never knew exactly where we went or what mischief we would get ourselves into when she sent us "out to play." All she knew was that I was supposed to look after my younger brother. The hill was a long walk of at least 12 blocks from our house. We just had to be careful when crossing the busy streets. I was riding my wagon and my brother rode his tricycle. We didn't have bicycles at the time. If we did, I was certain that we would have been seriously injured or dead going down that hill. When we reached the top of the hill, the sidewalk looked very steep and fast. We didn't know what to expect as we had never coasted down a hill so steeply inclined. The street levelled off just before reaching the traffic lights on Ontario St.

We started to coast slowly down the hill. As I was sitting low on my wagon, I could straddle my legs over each side and used my feet as brakes to slow me down. My brother on the tricycle had no brakes and he could only slow down by pushing down on the peddles to prevent the front wheel from turning too fast. The speed of our descent continued to increase as the hill got steeper. I felt that we were beginning to lose control, but I could still slow down using my feet. But my poor brother, being only four years old, was not strong enough to hold back the tricycle peddles from turning too fast. Halfway down, the pedals broke free from his feet and he and his tricycle blew past me as it ran uncontrollably down the hill. My brother was screaming and I could see the pedals whirling around wildly as the tricycle bombed down the hill. A thought flashed through my mind, "He was going to die!" There was a lot of traffic on Ontario Street and the tricycle was headed straight into the path of the oncoming cars.

Fortunately, my brother lost control when he tried to veer away from the traffic. This caused the tricycle to flip over, throwing Andy tumbling and rolling onto the sidewalk and stopping just short of the dangerous intersection. It was a good thing that my brother was short and small and very close to the ground. Other than a few scrapes and bruises, no bones were broken and he was fortunate not to have cracked his head on the sidewalk in his rolling around. He was lucky and I was luckier. A pedestrian came over to check him out. He said to me, "You kids shouldn't be coming down this hill like this. It's too dangerous!" But what did I know? I was just a kid. But maybe, I should have known better. Andy had some difficulties in walking as he was still hurting from his fall, so I put him on my wagon along with his tricycle and slowly pulled him back up the hill and then made the long walk back home. I got heck from my mother when she saw how bruised up Andy was. I just told her that he had an accident and he fell off his tricycle, conveniently ignoring the part about going down the big hill which we never did again. So, I could have lost a brother as well, but it didn't happen. With an older brother like me, who needed enemies! My father was right. It wasn't their time to go and I was very fortunate to still have my sister and brother around despite the reckless actions of my youth.

Story #7

LIFE IN A KITE!

Many people believe that money can buy you happiness. I don't believe this because of an experience I had with my father. I remember seeing him sitting on a lawn chair on the front porch of his Montreal duplex home. His legs were up resting against the railing and he was smiling and looking up in the sky. I looked up and I didn't see anything unusual, only blue sky and some clouds. I asked him, "What are you doing, Dad?" I then noticed that he was holding a large spool of string. He replied, "Flying a kite." "Where?" I asked squinting my eyes as I looked upwards. He pointed up and showed me this tiny little speck way in the sky about 400 ft. up in the air. "Wow", I thought, flying a kite so high from your front porch in the city! How did he even get it up there?

He started to tell me of all the times he flew kites in China and how he would have "kite fights" with his friends. He would take a piece of glass and crush it to finely sharp granules and then apply this glass coating to a glued section of his line. "You have to fly the kite higher than theirs." He said, "Then when the time is right, you pull very hard on your kite to make it dive downwards towards the other lines. You have to keep reeling your line in to keep the line tight enough to be able to cut the other lines like a knife." My father was beaming as he recounted his youthful experiences and reliving all his happy memories flying a kite. I could see that he was thoroughly enjoying himself.

When he brought the kite down, it wasn't any fancy or expensive store-bought kite. It was just made from split bamboo garden stakes covered with K-Mart plastic shopping bags and a tail made from cut-up newspaper. And it flew excellently! I learned from that day that you didn't need money to find happiness. My father never thought too much about money, and if it were meant for him to be rich, he said that he would find (note the distinction in the word "find" and not "buy") a lotto ticket in the street and it would be the winning ticket! He worked hard for his money and he spent it in pursuit of a good life with family and friends. Having money just gave him more options in what he wanted to do in life. It didn't necessarily make him any happier as the pursuit of money was never his primary purpose in life.

Now isn't that a very good life philosophy to follow? Seeing him smiling with contentment, I could see that he didn't need money to be happy. This incident had left a lasting impression on me.

Story #8

FAMILY SECRETS

E very family has skeletons in their closet. Things that were meant to be kept as secrets as they were either embarrassing or reflected poorly on their reputations. My father, Albert, had told me many stories of his early life in China, but there were a couple of stories he never told me nor any of his other children. Family secrets which he would have taken to his grave, yet he related these stories to my wife, Pat. He was very comfortable telling her these stories as he saw many similarities in the way my wife grew up, in poor and humble surroundings filled with hard work and sacrifices. Pat had to work immediately after high school to earn money, just like her older sister Shirley, to help their parents provide food, clothing and shelter for their large family with seven children. She would keep a little allowance for herself to pay for the tuition to attend evening courses at the local university. My father saw his daughter-in-law as a kindred spirit because of her commitment to do what was needed to maintain the well-being of her family. Besides, he liked her because she gave him his first two grandsons that would have made his father, Willie, proud to know that the Yep family lineage was intact. English was my father's second language and he rarely spoke to me in Chinese as my command of the language was barely passable, having been in Canada since the age of one year old. I had never been formally educated in Chinese. Pat, on the other hand, was fluent in his southern Chinese dialect and she understood the context that went with a language that could be so descriptive with few spoken words. Like my father, she grew up in China and she shared the same culture and traditions. His stories were always more colourful and descriptive in his native tongue. It was no wonder that he only shared these stories with my wife as he knew nothing would be lost in translation!

When Pat's grandmother was celebrating her 90th birthday, she had to go back by herself to Montreal to attend the big family party. We were living in Edmonton at that time. I could not go as I had to work and our sons were still attending high school. She was staying at my parents' place, and one late evening, he regaled her with amazing stories of his early life in China. This lasted well over three hours! Even though my father was born in Quebec, Canada, my grandfather, Willie, found it too expensive to raise a family there. He had too many children to feed. He decided to send his children back to China where he bought some farmland and built a large house for his family to live. Every dollar made in Canada back then was worth ten times more in China, and grandfather would regularly send money back to support his family there. He even took on a second wife in China to help raise his family. Yes, that was a perfectly acceptable practice to have more than one wife back then in China. His eldest son, Frank, stayed with him in Canada while his twin sons, Albert and Alfred, his fourth son, Dak Wing, and his daughter, May, were sent back to China along with his wife. My grandmother stayed a few years while her fifth son, James, was born in China, but she eventually returned to Canada, leaving her children to grow up in rural China.

Three more children, two daughters and another son, were born in Canada. Again, grandmother took them back to China where they grew up together with their other siblings. The Yep family was very large with nine children in total. My father, being the older of the twins, was deemed to be the eldest son in China even though he was really the second son in birth order. He had the responsibility to look after the well-being of the family. He always considered himself to be a poor farmer boy despite the money sent back from his father in Canada. Farming life was hard work and there was a lot of poverty in the rural countryside. He had to get up early every morning before sunrise to work in the fields and then attend school later on in the day. He had to make sure that that there was always enough food provided for his younger siblings so that they didn't go hungry. He never wanted them to be in a situation where they had to beg their neighbours for food. He and his twin brother were used to working hard every day and they never complained about it. The twins were very easy going, approachable and happy-go-lucky in their nature, always enjoying the simple things in life. This was where my father developed his belief that he didn't need to have money to be happy. He never pursued money just for money's sake. Family was always more important to him. The twins became very popular and they were well known in their village. Identical twin boys were very rare in China and they were seen as lucky charms. Being so auspicious, they were often invited to weddings where they had a reputation for giving everyone a great time in teasing and playing practical jokes and games on the poor bride and groom. They always did this in a fun way, making everyone feel entertained and happy at these celebrations. They often got a lot of good quality food to bring back home to share with their siblings.

He talked about the life of being a farmer and how he tried different things to consistently provide food on the table. Like his fishing exploits where he would string a net across the creek as this method would catch more fish than using a fishing pole. To earn more money, he had worked in a bicycle shop doing repairs in the nearby urban city of Sun Wui. There, he would also work as a bookkeeper as he was very proficient in using the abacus, the ancient Chinese calculator! He would talk about his local basketball team, the Flying Wings, that had this tall 6 ft. 3 in. giant centre coupled with the two speedy twins, Albert and Alfred, flying around on each wing. They were so good that they were invited to the city to play a professional basketball team from Hong Kong. For a poor rural basketball team played by farmers, they did very well almost winning the tournament. He recounted the stories when the Japanese invaded Sun Wui City and the neighbouring countryside. They had to flee very quickly from their house to find a safe place to hide. He and his twin brother had to carry their young sisters on their backs because they couldn't run fast enough to keep up. All these stories were exciting and mesmerizing to hear. Where was my mother, Judy, during all this time when my father told these stories to Pat? My mother was already fast asleep as she had gone to bed early. That was when the skeletons came out and my father recounted stories that had never been told to anyone.

The first revelation was that his younger brother, Dak Wing, didn't actually die of some disease while he was in China. That was the official story told to all family members. The reality was that Dak Wing was actually "stolen" when my grandmother with four of her children were sent back to China. The twins were about five years old, Dak Wing was three years old and baby May was about a year old. During the confusion upon arriving at the port city of Canton in southern China, it was fairly easy for some unscrupulous person to grab and kidnap young Dak Wing while Grandma Yep was busy and distracted looking after her daughter and all the luggage. She couldn't chase after the culprit when her son was grabbed, even if she wanted to. Male toddlers have been known to be kidnapped and then sold to others in China to keep family lineages intact. This must have been an extremely traumatic experience for my grandmother to lose her son, even though she committed no fault. This was definitely something she didn't want to be reminded of. So, the missing Dak Wing somehow "died" to explain his disappearance. Only the twins knew about this as they were there and they were old enough to understand what had happened. They saw the ensuing guilt and anguish experienced by their mother and later on, by their father when he found out. They kept this a secret from all their younger siblings, to honour the wishes of their parents while they were alive. It was only at this late night that the true story of Dak Wing surfaced and how there might be some long-lost descendants of the Yep family that we would never know. My wife had kept this family secret for a long time even after the eventual passing of my father.

The second revelation was even more startling. As my mother had already gone to bed, my father did not feel restricted by the presence of his wife. In China, arranged marriages were the norm and it was the traditional method used by all parents to retain a professional matchmaker to help find compatible matches for their prospective children. These matchmakers made it their business to know the eligible young people in their community, village or city. They would make the introductions to the parents, gather the relevant biodata of potential mates, and then consult with the Chinese astrology to confirm the compatibility of their matches. After that, they would negotiate and exchange financial gifts from the parents. In return, the matchmakers would receive handsome rewards for their services. My father's marriage to my mother was such an arrangement through a reputable matchmaker. His older brother, Frank, was the first son in the family to have an arranged marriage when he was sent back to China to get married. His parents, through a matchmaker, had arranged for him to marry a nice girl named Sandra, which he dutifully did. It was during his older brother's wedding that my father met Sandra's younger sister, a beautiful girl he fell instantly in love with. Apparently, the feeling was mutual! It was the proverbial "love at first sight!" The following year, it was my father's turn to get married. He wanted to marry Sandra's younger sister, but her parents were against it as they didn't want their two daughters to marry two brothers in the same family. Fate made sure that my mother became the second choice. She was not even my father's first love. No one knew this, not even my mother! How sad it was that life had to be so unfair to Sandra's younger sister. She never married after that. I only found out after my wife relayed this shocking story to me many years later.

Usually in arranged marriages, the matchmakers would try to match the prospective couples so that they would have complementary traits like age, education, appearance and social status. My father always considered himself to be a poor and simple person, not having or needing much to have a good life. My mother, however, was the youngest child coming from a well-to-do family and she lived in a large estate house with manicured gardens surrounded by an orchard of plum trees. She was used to getting her own way and living a pampered life where everything was given to her. Her parents spoiled her as the baby of the family and she was self-centred, valuing material things over family. Why would her father even consider or agree to let his daughter marry someone who came from a vastly different social background?

My father felt the same way when he was asked to meet and speak with his potentially future father-in-law. He had just recovered from an illness where he lost a lot of weight and he certainly didn't look too healthy. He couldn't see what my mother's father saw in him. Such a personal meeting was out of the norm as the matchmaker was supposed to be the go-between. My mother's father must have seen or heard something about my father that he wanted to confirm for himself. He wanted to be sure that my father would be that person who could take very good care of his daughter. As a parent, that was the best he could do for his daughter's future. He already heard that my father was industrious, resourceful and family-oriented. From the exploits of the twins at the weddings they had been invited to, he knew that my father was also fun-loving and gregarious and that people liked him a lot. These traits were the exact opposite of his daughter who he felt needed to know more about family values and responsibilities to compensate for her feelings of entitlement from living a sheltered life. In his wisdom, he considered my father to be a very good match for his daughter. Finally, my father was that rare Canadian citizen with the opportunity to go back to Canada in search of a better life. This prospect of a future life together in Canada was indeed compelling. It was the best arranged marriage he could have asked for.

The reputation of arranged marriages through the matchmakers have had exemplary results. In North America, the divorce rate was about 40% for couples who got together in the Western way, dating and choosing each other based on love, status and compatibility. For arranged marriages where the parents decided who their children would marry, the divorce rate had historically been a mere 4%! When my wife told me this story, it certainly made me better understand the context of my parents' relationship and how their differences actually made them stronger as a couple. I am glad it turned out this way as I might not have existed otherwise! Sometimes, things happen in life because they were meant to be as if Fate was on your side and the stars were in complete alignment. It certainly turned out that way for my parents.

Story #9

THE THINGS CHINESE EAT!

My wife, Pat, and I just completed a trip to one of our bucket list destinations – the remote and mysterious Machu Picchu. We took a land tour organized by Globus and this trip started in Cusco, Peru. While we were in this small ancient city, we wanted to try the local traditional dish of roasted guinea pig. This was supposedly a delicacy in Peru, but it can be an acquired taste. The restaurant made a big show of presenting the whole animal, head, feet and all intact, and decorated with a silly cap, before it was chopped up into smaller pieces to eat. The guinea pig looked like an oversized hamster which many people actually have as pets in North America. Nothing as appetizing as eating a critter with the eyes in its head staring back at you while you were chomping down on its thigh! Strangely, we expected this guinea pig to taste like pork, but it tasted like chicken! The skin, however, was quite tough and chewy. This little piggie should have been deep fried instead of being roasted. That way, the skin would be crispy, but then everything tastes delicious when deep fried! If you haven't lived on a farm or butchered any animals for food, you can be so squeamish eating a whole animal because all the meats we purchase at the supermarkets are so sanitized, cut up and packaged.

In all our travels, we have always tried the local cuisine whenever different meats are offered. I have eaten crocodile, emu, kangaroo, snake, sea turtle, Menke whale, the potentially poisonous blowfish, alpaca, buffalo, elk, horse, goat, rabbit and pigeon. I think I even ate cat once at my grandmother's place, but that was a long time ago. I don't remember what it tastes like other than it was kind of strange and greasy. It was definitely not chicken! I haven't eaten dog yet although I tried to do so when we were travelling to places in the Far East. I guess the Chinese do have a reputation for eating just about anything with legs (except a table), and dogs are no exception. I am quite adventurous in trying strange and unusual foods. I have no qualms in trying crickets and grasshoppers, and even worms and live caterpillar larva. Where I draw the line is in eating fertile embryo eggs. You know those eggs which the yolks are allowed to become half-formed embryos. Once, I had a bowl of soup placed in front to me and the eyes of the chick embryos were staring back at me! Totally gross! While supposedly another delicacy like the chicken claws, I couldn't eat them!

My father was a farmer back in China and when he came to Canada, he marveled at all the different breeds of dogs – the German shepherds, the terriers, the dachshunds, poodles, bulldogs, golden retrievers, etc. He said in China, there was only one type of dog, the eating kind! You might have seen this dog running around if you ever visited China. It was kind of big dog with short hair, either beige or black. One day, his dog on his farm disappeared and he suspected his neighbour caught his dog and ate it. I asked him why would he even say such a thing. He replied that if he caught his neighbour's dog on his property, he surely would have eaten it as well!

Chinese are generally stereotyped as being dog eaters which reminded me of a story regarding my youngest brother, Christy, who lives in a small suburb just north of Montreal. I guess he was the only French speaking Chinese living there. He was out in his backyard one day and his neighbour's small dog was constantly yapping at him. This happened whenever he was outside. It was very annoying to hear, and this dog's barking continued incessantly. I don't know why small dogs like to bark all the time as I have a neighbouring dog that barks at me every time it is out. His neighbour came out because of all the barking and my brother called her over to the fence to talk to her. He said to her in perfect French that if he ever caught her dog on his property, the dog will end up there – pointing to his BBQ. His neighbour looked at him with wide-eye horror and she quickly picked up her pet and ran back inside believing that this crazy Asian next door would really eat her dog!

She kept a good watch of her dog from that day on and she tried to keep it quiet. I guess being stereotyped did have some advantages. I don't know if my brother ever told his neighbour he was just kidding, but I do know for sure he has never eaten dog!

Story #10

THE BIG RAT

I remember one day while working with my father at the restaurant in Montreal. We were driving down this street, going to work. There was an open and empty field on one side and a row of those ubiquitous duplexes on the other side. All of a sudden, this really big sewer rat, almost the size of a cat, came out of the field and proceeded to run across the street. My father brought the car to a screeching halt in the middle of the road and he stared at the rat who stopped and stared right back. It was grimacing menacingly. This caused my father to jump out of the car, grab a crowbar from the trunk and he started to chase this big rat down the street.

He managed to corner it down one of the sloping garage driveway of a duplex house and he proceeded to beat the rat to death. I guess being a farm boy, he had absolutely no fear of rats, not even giant ones. He was making such a ruckus that the lady of the house came out to see what was the commotion, then seeing this strange Asian guy beating down and killing the rat. My father got up and looked at the dead rat, proud and satisfied at what he did. He proceeded to walk away at which point the lady exclaimed, "But, but what about the rat?!" My father simply looked at her and said, "Sorry, lady. That's not my rat." Then he calmly walked back to the car and waved to her as he drove on by.

I asked him, "Why did you kill the rat?" He said "That rat looked at me when it crossed the road and it showed me no fear or respect. I had to kill it. It was evil. If it didn't look at me, I would have left it alone." What does this tell me about my father? I am not too sure, but I know there aren't too many of us here that would be fearless enough to kill a rat the size of the guinea pig I once ate when I was in Peru! Maybe this rat would have tasted like chicken as well! Yes, Chinese will eat just about anything.

Story #11

WHAT REALLY MATTERS IN LIFE

I found the meaning of life. Really, I did. The question we need to ask ourselves is what makes our life worth living for. What are the things that really matter that will make us happy? We all know that one day we are going to die, and the fact we don't commit suicide means that there must be things in our lives that keep us going. It can be the love of your spouse, your children and family, your friends, fulfilment in your job, your possessions, your accumulated experiences, anything that left you with good memories and made you feel happy. Not to lecture you, but my father once told me that you don't need to be financially rich to be happy, although it certainly doesn't hurt. Wealth comes in many forms. We just sometimes fail to recognize it and forget to "count our blessings". When you do, you'll realize that your life is not that bad after all!

Balance in life means focusing on the things that will give you peace of mind. Work is a part of our overall balance, but it shouldn't be the most important and all-consuming one. Balance means accepting the things we cannot control or change over time. Things usually occur in our lives for no particular reason and sometimes beyond our comprehension. With this acceptance, we should try to remain positive and continue to do our best to make things better, a little bit at a time. This can only lead to a better life for us and for those we know.

Balance in life requires balance in your thinking. In our world of opposites, there are always two sides to every story or situation, like good and evil, love and hate, man and woman, with countless shades of grey in between. Diversity of thought leads to clarity in how we think, allowing us to make decisions based on our past events and future expectations. Balance is living in the present. This balance in life is the path to Happiness.

I would like to leave you with some thoughts which reflect the life philosophy of my father. He used to say:

Money isn't everything. You don't have to be rich to be happy.

It's not what you've got, it's how much you enjoy what you have.

Don't worry all the time. Be happy!

My father always thought the best of people, and he gave them the benefit of the doubt. He was always generous with family and friends. He believed in the good in people. And if you helped them, they would help you in return. He never really cared about money. Family and friends were far more important to him. He believed that the bonds created with family and friends had to be strong, because at the end, that's all we would have left. These bonds would ensure that the people you trust would be there when you need them and that they would do the right things for you. He was an optimist, always hoping and doing his best in everything he tried.

I learned a lot from my father, growing up with him. Sometimes it was difficult to follow his philosophies in life, as I got caught up with my own life struggles and changes. But that is what life is all about. Doing the best I could in coping with all the ongoing changes around me. Happiness is a frame of mind. It is a choice. Each of us has control over our daily lives and whether we look at things positively or negatively. There have been so many good things that we have experienced in our lives. All we have to do is to remind ourselves of the blessings we have received and not to take them for granted. Each of us know what we had hoped and expected our lives to become!

Story #12

WHAT MY FATHER NEVER TOLD ME

In the North American culture, it is normal and expected for parents to openly show emotions when raising their children. This is done by not only telling them that you love them, but also praising them, saying how proud you are of their achievements and by hugging them often. However, this was definitely not in the Chinese culture. My father never told me that he loved me and he never said that he was proud of me as his eldest son. He never showed me any expressions of affection like hugging me, or even patting me on the back. I was simply expected to be the best in everything I did and to always try to do the right things. These were sometimes very high and unrealistic expectations.

My wife, Pat, had always been perplexed at my constant search for some sort of validation or recognition for any of my achievements. I wasn't insecure. I just felt that I was missing something that would have made me feel better about myself. My mother was very similar to my father in this respect. There were no public displays of affection. When I was growing up, I never saw my parents holding hands or kissing in public. It was only later on when they became more "Westernized" that they would do a perfunctory kiss or hold hands while dancing at family gatherings like weddings and parties, as these social actions were the expected norm.

Come to think about it, Pat was like that as she grew up in Hong Kong. The Chinese influence and culture were much stronger in her. I had noticed that when our two sons, Ted and Tim, were growing up, she rarely hugged them or told them how proud she was of whatever they were doing. In her childhood, she was never praised for anything she did. She was expected to do well. She simply took personal satisfaction when she did things well! Chinese parents were accustomed in pushing their children to continually be the best at almost everything. They believed this was the path to success in life. But this pressure to succeed in all things could be relentless and stressful. It was also not realistic to be good at everything. Pat also had a hard time in giving me praise of any kind. She would say, "You already have a swelled head. Why would I want to make it any bigger!" But she slowly changed as our sons, being totally westernized, expected to be praised and hugged like all their friends were. We now do this regularly with our grandchildren. You would never understand why the Chinese customs were like this if you were raised in the North America way.

When I was growing up, I spent a lot of time with my father working at the restaurant. I started working there when I was only 12 years old, washing dishes, or as my father would say "playing with water!" when he saw how much fun I was having. I worked there for nine years learning all the various restaurant positions from busboy to waiter, host to front desk cashier, take-out service and caterer. I even learned how to cook the messy restaurant way! I worked the summers and week-ends there until I was 21 years old and had graduated as an engineer. This early restaurant experience shaped my character as I watched how hard my father worked and how well he treated people. Even though I never formally learned how to read or write Chinese and my spoken dialect was very rudimentary, I was continually exposed to the other Chinese workers at the restaurant. Over time, I learned what it was like to be Chinese and more importantly, to think like a Chinese. The Chinese cooks would often tease me by calling me "jook sing", or the North American equivalent of being a "banana" – yellow on the outside (looking very Asian), but very white on the inside (thinking and acting like a Caucasian)! The ironic part was that I was probably more traditional than a lot of Chinese especially when it came to family values and traditions. Working with my father allowed him to reinforce the Chinese customs he expected me to follow. He was the perfect role model for me.

As I was the eldest male of the next generation of the Yeps. I was expected to set a positive example for all future Yeps to follow in making the Yep family lineage stronger. I was also expected to take care of our immediate family when my father was gone. This would mean looking after my mother and to be there to help any of my siblings whenever they needed help. This was what my father would have done. Finally, I was expected to follow the ancient Chinese traditions of "filial piety": meaning to get married and have sons to continue the family line; to teach the children the importance of family; to try to fulfil any unrealized dreams or desires of their parents and to redress any of their past wrong doings or misgivings. My father somehow instilled all these values in me. My older sister used to bristle at the fact that so much importance was given to the eldest son and never to the eldest daughter. She would complain, "Who made you the head of the family?" I didn't have the answer then, but I have it now: "Centuries of Chinese tradition." True, it was unfair, but life doesn't have to be fair. You have no choice in life whether you were born male or female, the eldest or the youngest, or rich or poor. It is what it is. You can only control what you want to make of your life.

I was expected to honour my father and my mother and my ancestors. I did this for my father and his twin brother, Alfred, when I formally organized the big celebration of their 70th birthday in 1992. This party took a year to plan and I did it with the participation of my uncle's eldest son who was four years younger than me. This milestone event included not only the Yep family members were invited, but also all the extended families and in-laws and a few very close friends. In total, there were over 130 guests invited.

It was also very important to me that my eldest son, Ted, attended. Like myself, he was also the eldest male Yep of his generation. As such, he had the responsibility and role to set a good example for future generations of Yeps to follow. Ted, at that time, was very busy with exams at the COOP program at the University of Waterloo in Ontario. He had to take the Saturday off from his studies and travel to this special event. This meant taking a bus to Toronto and flying to Montreal and taking a taxi from the airport directly to the party. Then later on in the evening, leave the party early near the end of the banquet dinner to catch a flight back to Toronto and then a bus back to Waterloo very late that same day. My son had to experience and be part of this celebration to better understand these Chinese values and traditions.

Looking back at this party, it was a very special event and the things we did will never be repeated. I had mapped out the Yep Family genealogy and created a comprehensive diagram of the family tree with all the members names shown in both English and Chinese and the years they were born and died. I gathered all the old archival family photos and made a photo book master using the best ones. I wrote and recorded the history of the Yep family in Canada. It was very important to get all this information on paper while my father and his siblings were still alive. Those who have failed to do this risk losing their identities of who they were and where they came from.

My father was very artistic, especially in his brush-stroke Chinese calligraphy. I took his design of the Yep surname and I had it digitally reproduced. This image was made into logos used to make the rubber stamps, baseball caps, tee shirts and jackets which were to be given out as gifts at the party. When his siblings checked in at the party, they were surprised to get a drawing of the Yep Family Tree, a photo album of old family pictures, two rubber stamps with the Yep logo, and baseball caps with the Yep emblem (red and gold caps for his brothers and white and red colours for his sisters.) The Yep family legacy was preserved. By doing this, I had honoured both my father and our ancestors.

My father became a tennis bum in his retirement. He played tennis every day while his twin brother took up square dancing. My brother, Andy, organized a tennis tournament prior to the party. He and our cousin prepared a Yep questionnaire with strange and fun facts. My youngest sister, Sally, was a fashion designer and one of her dresses had won an award that was published in a magazine. Our niece, Suyin, modeled it during the party. Because my father and my uncle were identical twins, I created a slide show of their early photos asking the question "who was who?" They looked so much alike even their own children got them mixed up! Most people at the party couldn't tell the difference. There was music and dancing and many participated in karaoke singing. And of course, the 10-course banquet style dinner was excellent. The twin brothers had a tremendous time kibitzing with each other as they opened their gifts. They were very happy when their siblings surrounded them and they gave to each of them a pair of golden peaches which symbolized longevity and good life. Everyone was enjoying the party and having a great time. The Yep family had never been so close and they had never felt so united together as a family unit.

Near the end of the party, Uncle James, my father's younger brother, beckoned me to come over. He was sitting down, relaxing and he had this big smile on his face. He told me that his family was enjoying the party immensely. He acknowledged all the hard work I had done in organizing the party and for giving him such special mementos to remember this once-in-a-lifetime family celebration. Then out of the blue, he said, "Tony, you are a good son!" Wow! He said something my father had never told me! Maybe my uncle was hoping that one day his eldest son, Sandy, would honour him in the same way I had done for my father. By now, I had been exposed to the Chinese culture and I understood the context. I already knew that my father was proud of me. And my father knew that I knew too. In his own way, he loved me very much. He didn't need to say the words or do anything like openly hugging me or patting me on the back. I just felt it and the feeling was really good – one of satisfaction and being at peace with myself for having honored him. I needed nothing more. I was happy.

It's hard to explain this feeling that required no words or actions. I tried telling this to my sons, Ted and Tim, and all I got were blank looks. The context of these Chinese traditions is subtle and sometimes difficult to understand. Maybe one day my sons will understand these family values that my father instilled in me and my expectation for them to carry on this tradition with their own families. But I might have to be more forthright and just tell them, in the North American way! Direct and to the point! Otherwise, things will certainly get lost in translation!

Chapter 3

RESTAURANT STORIES

Story #13

CHINESE RESTAURANTS IN MONTREAL

When my great grandfather, Charlie, first came to Montreal, he started in the laundry business like most other Chinese immigrants. It was very hard work with long hours and he barely made enough money just to survive. Fortunately, he left the laundry business and he became a merchant selling goods to the Chinese community. This allowed him to make a better living for himself and his family. His son, Willie (my grandfather), was the one who eventually got the Yep family into the restaurant business. Four of Willie's five sons were directly involved being partners or working in various restaurant ventures. This started with the Nanking Café which occupied the top two floors in the landmark three-story building located on the corner of Lagauchetiere and Clark St. The main floor housed the Ho Ho Snack Bar which was very popular for those big and deliciously sweet butter rolls and the local Chinese gambling joint where my grandfather managed and operated. The building still exists today, but the restaurant that was started in 1933 by the Lee Family has long since been gone. My father and uncles started working at the Nanking Café when they first came to Montreal from China. They all initially lived at my grandfather's house which was only a block away from the restaurant in Chinatown.

Bill Wong was the first manager of the Nanking café and he was a Western educated person, having the distinction of being one of the very few Chinese to ever graduate with an engineering degree from the prestigious McGill University. But he found out very quickly that being Chinese limited his career opportunities as an engineer and that he could have better success by being an entrepreneur and restauranteur. He became the owner of the House of Wong Restaurant on Queen Mary St., serving the predominantly Jewish clientele in the Snowdon district of Montreal. The early Chinese immigrants came from the southern parts of China where Cantonese was the predominant language. Cantonese food focused on freshness in meats, fish and vegetables and it was not spicy, unlike the cuisine of the northern parts of China. The dishes were altered to cater to the North American palate which favoured deep fried foods with tangy and sweet sauces. The House of Wong became very well known for its delicious food and those unique open-ended and deep-fried eggrolls which their Jewish customers loved to eat. In the 1950s, this restaurant set the standards for Chinese food in Montreal. It also revolutionized the take-out foods by offering free local delivery. This restaurant was so successful, it led to the creation of his second and most well-known Chinese restaurant in Montreal, the iconic Bill Wong's (1963-2007) on Decarie Blvd. It became the city's first Chinese buffet restaurant, popularizing the "all-you-can-eat" buffets that have been copied by restaurants all over the world. The best Chinese restaurants back then were the Nanking Café, Ruby Foo's, Bill Wong's and the House of Wong.

Most Chinese restaurant businesses didn't survive as the people they hired as cooks and waiters were very transient, moving from one place to another whenever a better paying opportunity came up. Bill Wong's restaurants were the exception and they had longevity because he would offer his best people, including his cooks, minor shares in the restaurant they were working at in order to keep them there by making them part-owners. This was a very savvy business move. The Yep family were shareholders, or part owners, of both the House of Wong and Bill Wong's. All the people who worked there eventually branched off and started their own restaurant following the business model, cuisine and traditions set by the House of Wong.

Kenny Wong, no relations to Bill Wong, worked with my father at the House of Wong where they both learned the secrets of being successful in the restaurant business. Kenny married my father's younger sister, so there was a family connection between the powerful Wong clan and the obscure Yep family. Kenny had a very astute business mind, but he wasn't very people oriented. He had a fairly autocratic management style which expected people to follow his orders without question. When he decided to branch out and start his own restaurant, the two main partners he wanted were his older brother who was to be the head cook and my father who was to help him do everything else to manage and grow the business. My father was the perfect partner for him. Besides being smart and a very hard and reliable worker, he was very fair and supportive of the people who would work with him. People genuinely liked working for him. Kenny decided to locate the new restaurant in the pre-dominantly French speaking neighborhood in a small shopping center located in the east end of Montreal on the main Sherbrooke Street, serving the area between Pie IX Blvd and Lacordaire. Very few Chinese restaurants were located in that district. He even thought of giving his restaurant a distinctly French name by calling it Chez Wong. This was highly unusual as no Chinese restaurant in Montreal had even considered doing such a thing. Most Chinese restaurants had names like Silver Dragon, New Lotus Café or the House of Tom. As a matter of fact, there is probably a Silver or Golden Dragon restaurant in every major city in North America, that name being so popular! Despite this Francophone name, the French still had difficulties pronouncing the "W" in the Wong name, as the restaurant was often called "Chez Young".

Within two years, this restaurant became the best Chinese restaurant in the area. Their food was not only delicious, it was very reasonably priced. Those egg rolls that were beloved by the Jewish clientele at the House of Wong proved to be equally as popular and addictive to the French speaking locals. It certainly didn't hurt Chez Wong that it was the only Chinese restaurant in the area that offered free delivery on all take-out food orders. The take-out food business was simply fantastic. To demonstrate how busy they were, Mother's Day was usually the busiest day of the year and everyone had to come in to work on that day. They had six telephone lines just for taking orders for delivery, and the phones were fully lit up for six hours solid over the crazy busy supper time. They had their total complement of 20 full-time or part-time drivers doing delivery service, each taking 20 to 25 orders at a time. Every one of these delivery drivers made really good money in tips during that day. When I look at restaurants today, I haven't found another restaurant that busy with the volume of take-out orders requiring so many drivers working flat out over the supper hours. This was indeed a very special event, one that I had taken for granted how super busy the restaurant really was. Those were the good old days, well worth remembering.

Business was so good and the restaurant made so much money that it funded the building of Kenny's next restaurant. Similar to the way the Bill Wong built his signature restaurant from the success of the House of Wong, Kenny built his landmark restaurant, more traditionally named Kenny Wong, in the South Shore district of Montreal. Again, Kenny chose an area where there were few Chinese restaurants. This restaurant would offer the Chinese "all-you-can-eat" buffets that were made popular by Bill Wong. I remembered when this came out that you could get a dinner at the nearby McDonald's consisting of a Big Mac, fries and a drink for $5 and the buffet at Kenny Wong's was only $6 where you could gorge out on won ton soup, crispy egg rolls, dry garlic spareribs, prime rib, sweet and sour chicken, Cantonese chow mein and special fried rice. In no time, the business there also boomed. Imagine, competing with McDonald's and winning!

Don't get me wrong. Restaurant business has always been a tough business. If you didn't have consistently good food and service, the restaurant would not survive. The Chinese also had a strange concept of competition. Within a few years of success at Chez Wong, three other Chinese restaurants opened at the vacant corner lots kitty-corner and opposite the shopping center where Chez Wong was located. These competing restaurants thought that they could cash in immediately on the success Chez Wong had. But they were wrong and their food wasn't as good. These restaurants eventually closed the following year, one after the other.

I worked at Chez Wong when I was 12 years old until I graduated from university when I was 21. During that time, I learned every aspect of the restaurant business. I had many good memories working there in the summer time while making more than enough money to pay for my tuition at McGill University. I also had ample opportunity to practice and improve my French since most of the customers were French speaking. But my vocabulary was limited to ordering food in a restaurant. I found this to be quite helpful when my wife and I vacationed in France. When we went out to eat, I could order all sorts of food at their restaurants and we were never hungry there. However, the other conversational aspects of my French were not as proficient. It was quite normal to work six days a week in Chinese restaurants, 70 hours plus, consisting of four 10-hour days during the weekdays and 16 hour shifts on the Fridays and Saturdays on the week-ends. One day a week was an off day and it was usually during a less busy weekday. There was no such thing as a minimum wage or hours. I never had a week-end off and I had to work all holidays including Christmas and New Year days. Chinese restaurants were always open.

It was not always work, work, and more work at the restaurant. We did many fun things after work. I remembered finishing work late at 4 AM on a Friday night and instead of going home, I, and a couple of fellow waiters and cooks who were avid fishermen, would drive only one hour to the Long Sault area just at the Ontario provincial border. There, we would fish for the feisty and tasty smallmouth bass at dawn. It was in the early light when the fish were biting as they swam close to the shoreline to feed. We would fish at the overpass where the highway crossed the river and we would catch our limit of fish in less than one hour. Then we headed back home to get about four hours of sleep before starting our next work shift of another 16 hours on Saturday. Yes, we were young and crazy insomniacs back then. There was also the time I was working with my father during a weeknight. After closing up the restaurant at 2 AM, he decided that we (meaning the waiters and some of the younger cooks) should play some touch football in the lighted empty parking lot of the shopping center. My father always liked football and he fancied himself to be quite a good quarterback, capable of throwing a deadly accurate spiral football. We had a great time, but we were so noisy in the middle of the night, the people in the surrounding apartments, who had been asleep, called the police to stop us. It was a good thing that my father knew how to smooth talk the policemen. It also didn't hurt that these policemen knew my father as they had often frequented the restaurant for the egg rolls or coffee and he never charged them whenever they came. These were indeed very good memories.

Everything that you have experienced in your life becomes part of you. These events and the people you encountered will play a role in making you the person you are today. My restaurant years were very formative for me in showing what could be achieved through hard work, perseverance and a will to succeed by doing your very best. Of course, this included this little bit of luck that the Yep family didn't end up permanently in the laundry business!

Story #14

THERE IS NO PLUM IN THE PLUM SAUCE!

I hate to tell you this, but when you go to a Chinese restaurant, you are not eating authentic Chinese food! If you were invited for dinner at our place, my wife would not cook egg rolls, or crispy chicken, or sweet and sour pork, or ginger beef, or chow mein, or fried rice. These are the concoctions that the Chinese created in the restaurants to suit the palates of their North American customers. Instead, what you would have probably get are dishes like steamed whole fish with ginger and shallots, minced pork with salted fish and duck's eggs, plain stir-fried vegetables like bok choy, boiled chicken with oyster sauce and plain steamed white rice. There would be nothing overly sweet or deep fried. I guess you wouldn't want to come to such a dinner as real Chinese food might not be that appealing to your taste.

Everything at the restaurants usually taste fairly good because most of the dishes are deep fried, or accompanied by sweet and tangy sauces, or stirred fried in very hot oil in woks. Furthermore, they used a lot of msg (mono sodium glutamate) to make their foods and sauces taste better. Even McDonald's uses msg in their recipes. You can tell when too much msg is used as the food will be very tasty while eating it, but then you will always be very thirsty afterwards. Because msg is not good for you health-wise, it is used less now, but it is still used because of the trade-off in foods being tasty or healthy.

To further shatter your illusion on what you are eating at a Chinese restaurant, there is no actual plum in the plum sauce used to accompany the egg rolls. Thankfully, there is still egg in the egg rolls. I actually tried some commercially prepared plum sauce made from real plums. It wasn't very good as the taste was too tart and fruity. Here is the secret that most Chinese restaurants have known for a long time. Good tasting plum sauce was made using pumpkin paste. Considering that pumpkins are not regularly eaten in China, this "plum" sauce was made especially for the North American taste. Besides, it was much cheaper than using real plums which would be expensive to be made into a sauce, especially when the fruit was out of season. If you go to the grocery store today and check out the ingredients of a jar of plum sauce, you will see that the main ingredients will be pumpkin paste, water, sugar and vinegar.

This brings me to the next sauce, the red cherry sauce that is used on dishes like sweet and sour pork, pineapple chicken and fried won tons. There is no cherry used at all. The basic ingredients are water, sugar, vinegar, lemons and red food colouring, all thickened with flour or cornstarch. Sugar and red food colouring? Now that certainly doesn't sound too healthy! It looks like the inscrutable Chinese found a way to fool the unsuspecting Caucasian to eat anything deep fried and covered with a sweet and tangy sauce! If you want to try an easy and healthier version of a red sweet and sour sauce, but without the red food colouring, try the following recipe. It is excellent with fried won tons.

<u>Pineapple Sweet and Sour Sauce</u>

Two cans (400 ml) of pineapple tidbits.
Pour the juice in a sauce pan.
If you like pineapple in the sauce, add the tidbits from one can.
Squeeze the juice from the tidbits not used and add the liquid to the pan.
<u>Add:</u>   1/8 cup of white vinegar (the sour component)
         ¼ cup of Heinz ketchup (for colour!)
         1 tsp of dark soya sauce
         ¼ cup of sugar (brown or white)
         Juice of ½ lemon (optional)
Bring mixture to boil. Mix 3 tbsp of cornstarch with water. Thicken the sauce to suit.
Voila! Instant and tasty sweet and sour sauce with pineapple!

There was a popular and expensive dish at the restaurant called shrimp in lobster sauce. You guessed it! While there was real shrimp used (very difficult to fake or simulate shrimp), there was definitely no lobster in the lobster sauce! Real lobster was just too expensive to be made into a sauce. What you got was minced pork, chopped up black beans and garlic, all stirred fried and thickened with eggs. It still tasted very good despite having absolutely no lobster in it. People simply couldn't tell the difference, nor did they know any better about what they were really eating at the restaurants when it came to Chinese foods.

Having destroyed your perceptions of Chinese food, I will share the secret recipe for the egg rolls that were made famous in Montreal by such restaurants like The House of Wong, Bill Wong's, Chez Wong and Kenny Wong's. Other competing restaurants have copied their recipe and this version of egg rolls still exists today. These were the open-ended egg rolls originally deep fried in lard before being replaced by the healthier canola or vegetable oil. I got this recipe from my uncle George who was a chef, making the stuffing and sauce for thousands for these egg rolls. This recipe has been scaled down for home use, good enough to make about two dozen egg rolls.

Montreal Style Egg Rolls
Ingredients:

1 to 1-1/2 lb. minced pork
-tsp salt; tsp pepper; tbsp garlic powder, tbsp soya
  sauce, tbsp oyster sauce
1 medium cabbage (shredded)
1 tablespoon salt
½ teaspoon pepper
1 tablespoon sugar
3 eggs
1 package of egg roll wraps or skins

- Marinate the pork with the garlic powder, salt, pepper,
  soya and oyster sauce.
- Shred cabbage finely, sprinkle with salt to take water
  content out of cabbage.
- Refrigerate and drain excess water. Then thoroughly
  mix all the ingredients above.
- Roll in eggroll sized wraps leaving the ends open. Use
  water or milk to seal the edges.
- Deep fry the egg rolls preferably in lard. For a healthier
  option, use canola oil.
- When the egg rolls float to the top of the oil and look
  golden brown with the ends burnt, they are ready!

Plum Sauce
Pumpkin paste (200 ml or 6 oz)
Pineapple juice from 400 ml can of tidbits
Squeezed juice from unused pineapple tidbits.

Add:

1/8 cup brown sugar

1/8 cup vinegar

1 tsp garlic powder

1 tsp ginger powder

1 tbsp soya sauce

Dash pepper

Juice of 1 lemon (optional)

- Add ingredients in sauce pan and bring to boil.
- Corn starch thickener (3 tbsp mixed with water)
- Adjust ingredients to suit for taste and consistency

In my youth, I remember eating these crispy egg rolls smothered with plum sauce every day before I started my work shift at the restaurant. They were initially 15 cents each and after 10 years, they were 90 cents each. I would take a couple hot off the deep fryer, cut them lengthwise in half and cover them with the plum sauce that had no plums. Since they were fried in lard back then, it was grease heaven for me! The taste was heavenly, crispy on the outside, salty on the inside and tangy and sweet with the pumpkin sauce. I hope you are adventurous enough to try these recipes and taste for yourself these unique egg rolls that the Montreal Chinese restaurants were known for. They still taste quite good for deep-fried egg rolls, but probably less so because we don't use lard any more. What a pity. But the original taste will be forever etched in my memory.

Story #15

A LUNCH WORKING WITH RITA

My father always treated people fairly and with respect, regardless of who they were. He genuinely liked people and he would help them whenever he could. An incident came to mind that reflected his caring and generous nature. It was a weekday during the summertime, a normally slow day at the restaurant when few customers would come in for lunch. There was minimal staff that day, just my father, Albert, Rita, the waitress, and myself working in the front while only two cooks were working in the kitchen. Out of the blue, two bus loads of tourists pulled into the strip mall where the restaurant was located. Tourists usually didn't visit the east end of Montreal, so this must had been a special tour visiting the botanical gardens and seeing the Montreal Olympic facilities nearby. We were the only Chinese restaurant in the area and they must had heard about those big and tasty open-ended egg rolls that we were known for. Over 80 tourists descended on us all at once filling every one of the 35 tables we had, two to four customers per table. The tour guide noted that we had a luncheon special of soup, eggrolls, fried rice and chow mein with a choice of pineapple chicken or dry garlic spareribs, tea or coffee and dessert. Perfect! Specials for everyone! They needed to be served lunch quickly within the hour as they were on a very tight touring schedule.

My father was a super effective waiter in his earlier days before becoming the manager. When I was younger, he tried to teach me how to be efficient as a waiter, but I could never be as good or as fast as he was. I can still remember his words, "Tony, never go in or out of the kitchen empty handed." More often it was, "Tony, you are too slow!" Immediately, Albert took charge and he coordinated the work with Rita, who was very experienced and just as fast as Albert. "You take the orders and set the tables on this side," he said, "and I will cover the other side." I helped wherever I could, doing the busboy duties, initially setting the tables and bringing water out to everyone and then clearing the dishes and serving the drinks.

It was like a military operation with Rita and Albert running around like crazy in a chaotic yet organized way. The wonton soup came first, followed by those delicious eggrolls with plum sauce. Then the main course was served to each customer, followed by drinks and the home-made almond cookies for dessert. The food was delicious and the tourists ate everything with gusto. They were so impressed with the service they were getting. They didn't have to wait for anything. They left very good tips when they went back to their buses. After cleaning up, Rita brought all the tips to my father, expecting him to divvy it up. My father just smiled at her and said, "They are all yours. I was simply helping you do your job."

Rita was surprised and overwhelmed, but oh so happy! I have never forgotten the look of pure joy on her face. What she made in tips for just this one lunchtime was more than she would have made working three full days! My father was always this generous. Since this incident, Rita thought the world of Albert, and whenever he needed her help to cover for someone who couldn't come to work, Rita was there for him. I learned a valuable lesson that day. If you take care of your people, your people will take care of you! Consequently, when I grew up, I became a very people-oriented person in my management style. This care and focus on people have served me well in my own career in engineering and project management.

CHAPTER 4

OF MEN AND WOMEN

Story #16

"UNREALISTIC EXPECTATIONS"

I have heard many jokes in my time, but this one I will always remember. It reflects my expectations in life.

A husband and his wife were going to see the doctor. The husband was despondent and he was feeling very unhappy. Upon completing the examination, the doctor asked him to wait outside while he called his wife in to speak to her. "Your husband is suffering from a very severe stress disorder. If you don't do the following things, he will surely die."

"What must I do?" she asked, a bit apprehensively.

"Every morning, fix him a healthy breakfast. Be pleasant and agreeable at all times. For lunch, make him his favorite foods. For dinner, prepare especially nice meals. Pamper him. No chores. Let him do whatever he wants to do. And you do whatever he asks you to do. No nagging or arguing with him, no matter what. After all, he is always right. And oh yes …. one final thing, make passionate love with him several times a week and be sure you satisfy all his needs. Do this for a year and he will regain his health completely and find happiness."

The wife just looked at the doctor and she left his office without saying a word. Upon seeing his wife looking very solemn, the husband asked, "What did the doctor say?" The wife answered without hesitation, "He said that you are going to die!"

My wife loved this joke when she first heard it. No husband was ever going to get all this! Especially from her! However, from a man's perspective, the things the doctor said are perfectly reasonable to men. Man's happiness is very transparent and very simple, and if "the" wife treated her husband like that, all men would indeed be very happy. Yes, men can keep dreaming in technicolour! I used to think that the husband's happiness was tied directly to his wife's happiness. In the past, I've told many people that "Happy wife, happy life!" I don't believe in this anymore as there is too much emphasis on making the wife happy. Trouble is that while it is easy to figure out what makes men happy, the same cannot be said for what makes women happy. Tell me, what really makes women happy? This is not a rhetorical question. I really want to know. My wife always tells me what makes her unhappy, but this doesn't mean that removing all the things (and there are many) that make her unhappy will automatically make her happy. Such is the mystery of women to men. It may turn out to be a simple fact that if men are happy, women cannot be happy in our world of opposites. And the reverse should then be true for women … that if women are happy, then men should be happy for them! After so many years of marriage, I am not any wiser in this respect. Life goes on.

Story #17

FIRST IMPRESSIONS

Do you remember what it was like to be in love? Do you remember what your first impression was when you met your soulmate? One summer when I was visiting Pat's younger brother, Frank, he was dating Kate. I had invited both of them out for lunch. At the restaurant, I could tell that they were very much in love. They kept looking at each other's eyes, holding hands and casually touching affectionately. I felt like an intruder in their world. I might as well have been invisible to them. It was very sweet to see them so much in love. I wondered when was the last time I felt such intense emotions. It reminded me of the first time I met Pat. My best friend, Robin, whom I knew since elementary school, was dating Pat's older sister, Shirley, at that time. He invited me to a party where he intended to introduce me to Pat, hoping that we might take a liking to each other. When I first saw her, she was a vision of beauty! I even remembered what she wore at the party, fashionably dressed in a pure white outfit with matching white hosiery and shoes. She looked every bit like a heavenly angel. My first impression was, "Wow, this girl is way out of my league! I have absolutely no chance." Talk about a complete lack of self confidence! In life, sometimes all it took was a bit of luck. Before I go on, I must say for the record that I later told Pat, now my wife, that she was the lucky one for choosing me! And that I no longer thought that she was too good for me! She just smiled when I said this, as if she knew better!

I was quite a shy and introverted person in my youth, quite the opposite of the person I have become today! If you were expecting me to actually ask a girl out for a date, well, that would never happen. I had no confidence with girls then. It was a good thing that Robin was a lot more outgoing and sociable than I was. He had been thinking of taking a trip with Shirley to New York City. Why not have Pat and I go with them? I didn't know what Pat thought of me when we first met, but it couldn't have been too bad. It also didn't hurt that I had a car and we could all drive there from Montreal. I never realized how lucky I was that my father had bought me a car when I was in my second year in university. Even though it was a used car, a dark blue 1966 Plymouth Barracuda with that unique domed glass rear window, it was still all mine! I was one of few in university who actually had a car, and my father paid for the whole thing including my insurance. He didn't buy a car for any of his other children, only for me because I was the eldest son in the family. I just took all this privilege and favouritism for granted. Little did my father know that this car made it possible for him to get his eventual daughter-in-law who would give him his first two grandsons.

Surprisingly, at least for me, the sisters agreed immediately as they had always wanted to visit New York City, the Big Apple. Plans were made and we could even spend a full week there at a friend's apartment as they were conveniently away that week. We had a great time sight-seeing in the city visiting places like the Empire State building, the Statue of Liberty, the then World Trade Center and Central Park. We even saw the famous Rockettes at the Radio City Music Hall. This trip probably consolidated whatever impression Pat had of me, that maybe on a remote chance, I was worthy of her attention. It was a wonderful and memorable trip. We dated regularly after that and later on, I did find out from Pat what her first impression was of me. "Nice and safe," was her curt answer. Nice and safe!!! That's not what guys wanted to be known for! Handsome, stud-like, suave, smart, strong, a real catch were descriptions that I was hoping for. But I guess only mothers would think of their sons that way. In hindsight, I guess I was kind of quiet and nerdy back then. Pat would say, "Only kind of nerdy?!" Well, at least I made some sort of a positive first impression when it counted and I did find my soulmate. There definitely was truth in the quote: *"There is only one chance to make a good first impression."* We both had that chance to make a good impression and somehow the stars aligned and karma was on our side!

Years later, I wondered how was it possible that Pat's parents would allow their two unmarried daughters to go with two single guys, one whom they had not even met, all the way to New York City and then to stay together in the same apartment for a week. For a long while, I just thought that maybe her parents were very liberal minded. It never dawned on me that it was kind of unusual that we picked the sisters up at a pre-arranged place instead of at their home. The females reading this story would say, "You sure were a dumb guy! It was so obvious!" Truly, I was clueless. Pat simply said that they never told their mother! Shirley and Pat were already working then and they had taken a number of trips together to various cities during holiday week-ends and vacations. When they told their mother that they were taking a week's trip to visit New York City, she just assumed that her two daughters were going on another trip together. There was no mention whatsoever of these two other guys travelling with them! Such cunningness! They were truthful, yet very sneaky! But my best friend and I couldn't have been happier with the outcome, as we ended up marrying them!

I have since wondered what women really wanted in life, or more specifically, what made my wife happy? The old saying, *"Happy wife, happy life!"* couldn't work if you didn't know what happiness was to her. I could always tell what made her unhappy from the things she would complain about. But eliminating the things that made her unhappy was no guarantee in making her any happier. There were always so many others things to complain about. I thought that I had this genetic flaw which prevented me from understanding women. It was a reasonable excuse for my being so clueless. From my perspective, she got everything a woman would ever want – a big house, a lovely garden, her own car, a walk-in closet full of nice clothes, a sewing room for her hobby, two wonderful sons and four delightful grandchildren, a supportive family, great friends and most importantly, a loving husband who would do almost anything for her! Many times, I would ask her "Are you happy, Dear? Really?" She would look at me and give me that little smile of hers and say, "Don't you know?" In truth, I really didn't know. Women were such mysteries to men. Maybe they did this on purpose to confuse men.

In my naivety, I once thought that I <u>knew</u> what women wanted in life. I was so proud of this new found knowledge. I brashly told people this "secret" that, "Women wanted to be loved. They wanted to be appreciated and to be taken care of. Lastly and most importantly, they just wanted to be understood." Then I realized there was a deep flaw in my logic based on my belief that paradoxically, women who could be understood simply did not exist! At the end, the logical conclusion had to be that no one knew for sure what women really wanted because it was meant to be like that! Still confused? Well, join the club!

Recently, Pat and I were watching this Academy award winning documentary movie "Free Solo". It was the story about Alex Honnold who became famous by being the only climber in the world who in 2017 successfully scaled free solo up the sheer face of the daunting El Capitan peak at the Yosemite National Park. Free soloing meant climbing the mountain without the aid of any ropes and safety equipment. This meant that any slip or mistake would result in a fatal fall and instant death falling to the rocks below. Mountain climbing was already very dangerous even when done with all the safety equipment. There was a poignant and very revealing scene when his girlfriend, Sanni, asked him why he was so obsessed with climbing the mountain in such a risky and dangerous manner to the point of putting his own life and everything he had, including her, at jeopardy if he failed.

It was obvious that they both loved each other, yet this was not enough for Alex. She was afraid that she was going to lose him. She could not understand why it was so important for him to climb that damn mountain. Alex was very stoic in his response when he told her that climbing this mountain was something he had always wanted to do because no one had ever done it before. And he felt that he was one of the very few who could actually do it if he did his very best. If that wasn't good enough, and he failed and died as a result, that was still okay. He would have at least tried to do his best. What he could not do was to climb cautiously with the fear of falling stuck in his mind, trying to be safe all the time. He had to be absolutely focused on being fearless and perfect in his climb with no thoughts of failure whatsoever. Sanni could still not understand why, but she instinctively knew that unless Alex climbed this mountain, he could never be happy. I understood exactly what Alex was saying.

Men have this inner urge to accomplish things worth remembering, or doing something that would leave some sort of legacy of their existence. Maybe the male ego is driving this innate urge to be the very best in whatever men chose to do. It certainly provided an answer to my wife's question why it seemed so important for men to write their memoirs when they retired. Men are driven to achieve things. Then the epiphany of what women really wanted in life hit me. Most women will choose their mates with safety and security in mind – someone who would be a good provider and look after his partner. Sanni got her wish only after Alex successfully climbed El Capitan. Her life was now safe and secure, and she was extremely happy with the outcome despite the anxiety and trauma she had to endure.

It would be interesting if we asked the young women of today (generation X plus) what they thought of this "safety and security" issue with their potential mates. In hindsight, Pat's first impression of me being "safe and nice" suddenly made much more sense! For her, I seemed to have met her criteria for safety and security. After all these years, I am finally less confused!

Story #18

THE SUPERIORITY OF WOMEN

I was watching television one day and for some unknown reason, I ended up on one of those educational TV channels. I was ready to switch to something more intellectual, like Baywatch, when the show host announced that today's documentary was, "Why do men have nipples?" It sure caught my attention. So, I watched the show and what a revelation it was!

This documentary was very scientifically based presenting the truth with no "fake news". It revealed that while men had nipples, they really didn't have any need for them. They were extraneous. It turned out that the basic building block for all the human and animal lifeforms was in the female form, hence the nipples. This meant that all men started off as female. The key distinction here was that since everything started from a basic female form, then logically, the female model had to be the dominant form. This also meant that from a biological perspective, women were indeed superior to men! And that men were just variants of the basic female form! To take this logic even further, God in reality, should have been a female and all this man-made history and multiple religions got this wrong! This scientific and biological evidence cannot be refuted, but for some men, this might be too much to accept. What a conundrum these useless nipples have made for men.

I've also come across more disturbing evidence that besides being the dominant form, women were actually smarter than men. I had long-held views that smart children came from smart mothers. There is nothing scientific to substantiate this belief, just anecdotal evidence. I have a friend who is one of the smartest engineers I know. He has two extremely intelligent kids who became doctors. He thought it was because of his superior genes. Sorry, but that didn't compute with me. While he might have contributed to some miniscule effect, it was his wife that had the superior intelligence and the larger contribution! I always considered his wife to be smarter than he was. My son told me that from his medical studies, the intelligence traits came from the X chromosomes. And we all know that women are made up of X-X chromosomes while men are X-Y chromosomes. Do the math! Women would inherently have twice the intelligence genes than men! This was a proven biological and medical fact. Women had twice the potential to be smarter.

Some of you may have heard of Tom Peters, the modern-day guru of leadership and management theory. I heard him speak years ago, and this recognized authority said that in leadership qualities, women outscored men in 18 out of 20 categories and in the last two, men were only marginally better. Women listened better, they were less rank conscious, more self-determined, more trust sensitive and intuitive. They were inherently flexible and more naturally inclined to empowerment. They were not as power centric as men and they readily accepted ambiguity to name a few of these positive traits. And I might add, better looking than men!

You might ask then, why aren't there more women in high powered business places and government? There were some, but it is still a man's world. The answer might be that since women are inherently smarter than men, they "let" the men run the businesses and governments in the world. Why take on all the added stress and hardship working so hard for career and country? That is why men have generally died earlier than women! These career goals might have been important to men, but apparently, they were much less appealing to women. It was a very good strategy to let the men work themselves to death and then reap their rewards when they died! See how smart women have been? It may be a given that women might be superior to men in many ways! In hindsight, I think my wife's idea in not setting a career goal for work other than to retire early, doing only what she enjoyed doing, actually began to make sense!

But let me, as a man, have the last word on this matter, regardless of any perceived "superiority" of women. I will concede that Pat is smart. I might even go so far as to suggest that she is even smarter than me. **After all, she did marry me!** Such a smart woman! I hope she never regrets it!

Story #19

MIDDLE OF THE WAY

This poem, written by Carlos Drummond de Andrade, is about Life:

"Middle of the Way"
In the middle of the way, there was a rock.
There was a rock in the middle of the way.
There was a rock.
In the middle of the way, there was a rock.

Translation: Life will always be full of obstacles, and rocks will be in the middle of your way. You don't have to walk into them and be stopped. Go around them, jump over them, or push them out of your way, but don't let them stop your journey. You become the person you are by how you deal with the many obstacles you will encounter in your life.

There is a complementary quote from Alfred d'Souza on Life:

"For a long time, it had seemed to me that Life was about to begin – real Life. But there was always some obstacle in the way, something to be got through first, some unfinished business, time still to be served, a debt

to be paid. Then Life would begin. At last, it dawned on me that these obstacles were my Life."

This is kind of a pessimistic way of looking at life as a constant struggle filled with obstacles. But it is true. Then I realize that even though I may think that my wife is occasionally one of these "obstacles", she really is my Life. The journey of life can be a wonderful trip. It's a matter of attitude, seeing the cup half full and not half empty. Instead of seeing obstacles, consider them experiences to be lived and enjoyed.

STORY #20

YIN AND YANG

I have long struggled in my attempts to understand women. I still haven't figured out how they think. Why couldn't they just think like men? It would be a much simpler world! I did some research in determining what these psychological differences were between men and women. There were some noticeable parallels between the Chinese philosophy of "Yin" and "Yang" and the characteristics associated with the way our "left brain" and "right brain" were supposed to work.

Left Brain	**Right Brain**
Logical	Intuitive
Details oriented	Big picture oriented
Facts	Imagination
Practical	Spontaneous
Analysis	Feeling
Status quo	Creative
Math and sciences	Philosophy, fine arts

Yin	**Yang**
Feminine	Masculine
Yielding	Aggressive
Emotion	Reason
Negative	Positive

Yin	**Yang**
Darkness	Light
Cold	Warm
Moon	Sun

As an Engineer, I had been trained to be left brain oriented being logical and fact-based. However, I was also fairly adept in right brain thinking, being creative and able to see the "big picture". Some might say that I was in touch with my feminine side! I always felt that I was sort of "different" in my thinking, and that my thought process was sometimes strange. As my wife would say, "Only sometimes?" I wondered about the vastness of the universe, the meaning of life, why were we here, why people did the things we do to each other and does anything we do really matter, where do we go when we die, and why women are always so hard to understand!

One could say that men tend to be left brain oriented, the logical and reasonable side; whereas women tend to be right brain oriented, the emotional and intuitive side! This would explain why most of the time, I would not know what my wife was thinking about! I liked the ancient Chinese philosophy of Yin and Yang for its comparison of women being like the dark and mysterious moon while the men were the light and the sun! This meant that a woman's life would revolve around her man. Pat had frequently said that I had such unrealistic expectations! She also said that there should have been an added category of "Dumb and Smart", and guess who got to be in the dumb column!

Story #21

OXYMORON – THINKING OUT OF THE BOX!

Before I go any further, let me conduct a simple test to see whether you are left brain or right brain oriented in your thinking, as described in the previous story "Yin and Yang." You might already know that engineers and scientists tend to be left brain logical thinkers. But that doesn't mean that they are devoid of any right brain creative activities. You can conduct this test on anyone. It was something I picked up from the many leadership courses which I had taken. Unlike the Myers-Briggs test which tried to characterize your basic personality into four distinct types – whether you were introverted or extraverted, a thinker or a feeler, or sensory or intuitive, and whether you were judgmental or a passive observer - this test focused solely on your left or right brain tendencies.

The Test Question:
In the house or apartment where you are living in, count all your windows. Go ahead, do it now. Whatever you consider to be a window, count it! Don't read further! Done? How many windows are there?

Now the answer to this question is not the number of windows you came up with. The actual number of windows is irrelevant. The real question is where were you when you were counting the windows? Were you inside the house, outside, or both? People who counted the windows from the inside tend to be left brain oriented, walking from room to room and looking at the details. People who counted from the outside tend to be right brain oriented as they were the creative conceptual thinkers. Some counted the windows from both the inside and the outside of the house. This demonstrated a balanced thinker using both the left and right sides of their brains equally. I remember when I first did this exercise, I was sitting way back at the far corner of my backyard looking at the entire outline of my house and counting the windows from the outside. Even though I loved the details because of my engineering training, I was also artistically creative and I could see the big picture and think of possibilities others could not see. I had to purposely learn those activities that were right brain oriented to balance my thought processes.

Engineers tend to be such linear thinkers as they are mostly left-brain oriented. It is an oxymoron if you think engineers can think "out-of-the-box" because most of them can't. To have balanced thinking, the "creative" right side of the brain has to be used — things like writing, artwork, music, literature and philosophy. The "logical" left side of their brains dominate with thoughts and actions based on math and science. Engineers see most things in black and white, with very few shades of grey, as public safety demands that our work and designs must always be safe. You put anything written in front of engineers or share an opinion or idea that doesn't seem logical or correct, and they will tell you immediately what is wrong or what does not make sense, and what you need to do to correct it. Engineers are trained to spot problems and to fix them. This trait, unfortunately, is in the DNA of all engineers. They can't help themselves in telling people when others are wrong! Not because they think that they are always right, but because they believe that they have been trained to do only the right things! Most times, engineers don't even know that they behave this way. Maybe that was why Pat had felt on many occasions that I was a very inflexible and difficult person to live with! But now, I have a good excuse to say that it is not my fault as my training as an engineer makes me do the things I do! Nice try! I still haven't figured out why women think that they are always right, when they are not even engineers!

What does all this mean? Nothing much other than an interesting exercise to make people think about themselves. There will always be exceptions to the rule with people maximizing the full potential using both sides of their brain to become awesome thinkers!

Story #22

JUDGE JUDY

An oxymoron is defined as "a figure of speech that uses seeming contradictions, such as cruel kindness." Could a "logical woman", or a "woman that can be understood" also be examples of an oxymoron? If they are, then there is one woman I admire because she embodies the very meaning of this oxymoron. I can always understand her completely. She is Judge Judy! You may have seen her top-rated TV show where she is the judge in a small claims court setting. This show supposedly uses real people in actual cases suing each other for all sorts of reasons. Mothers suing daughters, husbands against wives, friends against former friends, tenants against landlords, neighbours against neighbours and how they would openly cheat and lie to get their ways. I don't know where the show finds all these dishonest people with no integrity or moral values, but apparently there are lots around. Unfortunately for these people, Judge Judy knows how to spot the liars and cheaters and she is very good at catching these people in their lies and making them appear to be so ignorant and stupid in front of millions of her TV viewers. My wife said that these couldn't be real people, but some of the things said and done are so outrageous that they could only be done by dumb people! No real actors would want to take the role of looking so foolish and being seen as the stupid one.

Judge Judy is a very intelligent and logical person. She puts more emphasis in reasoning and facts over conjecture and personal feelings. I always understand her reasoning and what she says. I can't say the same for my wife who at times has driven me to distraction with her brand of "logic", insisting that whatever she believes to be true is the truth! After being a family court judge for over 30 years, Judge Judy is extremely good at what she does, mainly her skills in judging the character of people to determine those who are telling the truth and those who lie on purpose. Her logic is like that of an engineer who must deal with facts to arrive at proper decisions. No unsubstantiated speculations, and no hearsay (the legal term for gossip) affect her decisions. Like some of my skilled engineering colleagues who are experienced enough to spot an error by just looking at a drawing or document, she is very adept in finding the truth. She is always right!

Judge Judy is a human lie detector. She asks the people to always "look her in her eyes" when she questions them. With her laser-sharp memory, she remembers everything they said. Then she thoroughly checks to see if their verbal statements matched with their written testimonies. Then questions come in rapid succession to try to catch them in a lie. First came the easy ones like where do you work, for how long, and when did you buy the car. Then came the hard ones like why do you think the money given by your mother was a gift and not a loan? If they could answer all her questions without any hesitation while looking directly at her, then the likelihood was that they were telling the truth. Judge Judy said that *"When you tell the truth, it comes out very easily and you don't have to think about it."* Every time a person's eyes move about or look away, or there is hesitation in the answer, she knows that the person is thinking of ways to avoid the consequences. In other words, that is lying and why face-to-face conversations are so powerful when seeking the truth! I have learned a lot about human nature just watching Judge Judy. I still don't understand why people would purposely choose to break up their families, friendships and relationships, or to compromise their integrity and morality, because of money and their selfishness.

There is a quote from Alexandre Dumas:
"Do not value money for any more or less than its worth. It is a good servant, but a bad master."

Having money means you have more options about what you can do with your life. But if your life is mainly consumed by the pursuit of money and possessions at the expense of family and integrity, then this could lead to bad outcomes in your life. Still there are many people who believe that only money can buy them happiness.

I used to think that all women were difficult to understand, especially to men. I can no longer say this with any certainty because of Judge Judy! Some women are very logical and they can be understood! Now if only men can read women's minds, that would be so wonderful not to have to figure out what they are really saying!

Story #23

ON COMPATIBILITY

Have you ever noticed that people who have been married or partners for a long time are rarely 100% similar with each other? They will have varying differences in their personalities, skills and capabilities. For example, I would say my wife, Pat, and I are only about 50 to 60% compatible at best. We have enough things in common that will keep us together such as our love for travelling, time spent with our grand-children, and our bonds to our families and friends. Our personality differences are quite noticeable. I am the incurable optimist and she is a realist (she doesn't like it when I call her a pessimist). I don't mind trying something different at least once, things like bungee jumping and sky-diving which my wife would never even consider doing. I like managing and interfacing with people and she likes managing things and not people. I don't know why she includes me as one of these "things" she likes to control! She seems to enjoy telling me what to do! I thrive in confrontational situations with problems to solve, but my wife tries to avoid them whenever she can. I liked to bargain for things as I hate to pay full retail price for anything. My wife waits for things to go on sale, or if bargaining is needed, she will ask me to do it.

We know another couple whose wife's personality traits were similar to mine. The two of us were focused and driven by our work life. We were very good at managing people and situations, aggressive, articulate, extroverted and career driven. We were very comfortable in our leadership roles, and we could easily give presentations and speak in public whenever needed. Meanwhile, her husband was more like my wife, relaxed and easy going. Work was never a career priority for them. Family and other things were more important. They were definitely hardworking, but not confrontational and they enjoyed being somewhat introverted. We had this standing joke that if my friend's wife and I were married, we would be these highly successful consultants, working and travelling the world, never retiring because we loved our jobs so much. We would most likely be very rich, but with no time to start a family. We would be constantly competing with each other to see who was more successful. We would also be dead by now!

There is a reason why we don't choose mates too similar to ourselves. Successful couples have complementary skills and personalities. You may have seen the movie Jerry McGuire where Tom Cruise said to his wife, played by Renee Zellweger, *"You complete me."* Successful couples that stay together are never 100% alike. Those couples who are too much alike are probably separated or divorced right now. It is more like 50-70% compatible, enough to see things in common and be attracted to each other, but still different enough to make life interesting. You will have traits that your partner will not have. That is why opposites do attract. Together, the sum of the traits will always be greater than from just one individual.

Contrary to what men think about their prowess to woo and to pursue the person they are after, it is the woman who actually picks her mate. A wise woman will select the mate who will love her and care for her. But equally important, her mate will have the skills which will complement hers, "to complete" them both as a couple. My wife probably saw in me the ability to make a good living and life for our future family, to take care of our financial needs, and to manage all the things that she couldn't or didn't like doing, like bargaining, writing letters of complaints, taking care of house and car repairs, negotiating with contractors, arguing with people and bureaucratic corporations, dealing with ever changing technologies and even programming the VCR! She dislikes the constantly changing technology. That is why I think I was her chosen one! Simple enough, but sometimes, I think she questions whether she made the right choice! I was definitely not the most "studly" person she met (more like "dudley" as she would say), but I was honest, logical and pragmatic, hard-working and career-oriented, fully capable of caring for her and our eventual family. I was also very black and white and relentless (like a pit bull) in pursuing things which I perceived to be the right things to do. I liked to talk (maybe a bit too much) and I was very good in communications and written documentation, skills used to fight city hall, bargain with people and manage people and projects – all the things she didn't like doing.

In order for me to survive and to be good at what I did, I had to improve my verbal and written skills. I didn't let people take advantage of me, and I tried to be the best person I could be in engineering, project and people management. I had a very successful career as an engineering and project manager. I was used to telling people what to do because I was good at it and I rarely made mistakes. This attitude really caused my wife grief when I first retired as she didn't like me constantly "getting in her way." She saw me as a disruption to her set routines, trying to control her life and telling her what to do, like expecting to have a hot lunch every day and on time! Did my work career change me? Most likely. Were they bad changes? Depends on who you are! My wife insists that I wasn't the same person she married. But then who is? As I got older, I found that I became less tolerant of people who did stupid things and less patient with life issues which wasted my time. I didn't take crap from anyone, which sometimes unfortunately included my wife! There seems to be a lot more ignorant people nowadays. She tried to change these negative traits of mine which had worked well and were necessary for me to succeed in my work life. However, they were definitely not useful in maintaining a harmonious relationship with one's partner in retirement. Being the stubborn guy I was, I even told her that if she didn't like what I did or the person I have become, then deal with it. After all, she did choose me knowing exactly who I was and I wasn't going to change! While this might have seemed to be a logical and reasonable thing for me to say to her, I caution all my male readers, this was not a smart thing to say to your partner, unless you like sleeping on the couch! I say this from experience, so don't be as reckless as I was.

Ironically, the very traits that were seen to be positives in your early years of marriage may become the very source of conflicts in your later life. The good friend who I was so fortunate not to marry instead of my wife, was also an excellent social worker in her career. She told me that as we aged and go through the various stages of our lives, the very traits that brought couples together in the first place, will be the same traits that will drive the couples apart in their later stages in life, especially during retirement when couples are living together 24/7. Every idiosyncrasy and minor irritant that we had previous not noticed or had ignored became magnified and troublesome. The toilet seat left in the upright position became a big issue! Silly little things. In order for the marriage to survive, we had to learn how to become couples again. This was difficult, because as we aged, we got fixated and set in our ways. We didn't see anything wrong in who we were or what kind of person we had become. We didn't acknowledge that we had changed, sometimes for the better, but many times for the worse. My wife and I needed to concentrate on the positive things we liked to do together and what made us a couple in the first place. It is a good thing that we do have grandchildren as I cannot be that "difficult" person my wife thought I was. I had to be patient and understanding and positive around the little ones.

So far it has been working. Life is never that simple, and it is neither black or white. There are so many shades of grey. And Life doesn't have to be fair. It is what we choose to make of it and we have to work to keep our relationship on solid footing. I am fortunate, indeed, to have found a partner who is my "mate for life". I trust that you are likewise as fortunate in the selection of your special partner. Remember that relationships are like life. We need a bit of challenge in our lives to make us feel alive!

Story #24

"ANDO AND DATING"

I heard this joke while travelling to Shanghai in China. Our tour guide, whose name was Ando, was this energetic, reasonably good-looking young Asian guy who was telling us what the dating scene was like trying to date the many beautiful, chic and fashionable ladies in this cosmopolitan city. Shanghai is considered to be the Paris of China. Why he was telling this story to the tour group instead of describing the local sights and scenery was beyond me, but it is worth re-telling! By the way, all of this was done in Cantonese, and my comprehension of this dialect is quite poor, even with my wife's help in recounting this story. I hope I didn't lose too much in the translation.

Ando was from the countryside when he first moved to Shanghai and he was wary of his first date as he heard that the women in the cities were very sophisticated and demanding. Anyone who has visited China knows what the traffic is like and how dangerous it is to simply cross a busy road. Cars have been known to ignore traffic lights and speed up to drive pass the pedestrians even while they are crossing the street on a green light. When he and his first date came to a street with the red light showing, he naturally stopped and waited. His date, however, didn't break stride and walked into the oncoming traffic, skillfully dodging one honking cars after another, laughing and skipping all the way to the other side. The light changed to green and Ando crossed the road and upon reaching his date, he was greeted with a "SMACK!" Right across the face! "What a wimp!" "So afraid of cars to cross the road!" she exclaimed, "I would never go out with such a cowardly man!" Well, so much for the first date.

Soon afterwards, Ando was fortunate enough to get himself a second date, and by chance, both came to this same street crossing, and the light was again red. Ando remembered his previous experience and he didn't want to repeat it. He wanted to impress his date and show her how brave and fearless he was. Without hesitation, he jumped onto the road, narrowly dodging several cars bearing down on him and somehow made it to the other side amidst all the noise of honking and screeching brakes from the cars swerving madly to miss him. He waited on the other side for his date to join him. He had a smug smile on his face, as he was so proud of what he had done! When she did join him ….. "SMACK!" Right across the face! "What a reckless and foolhardy person you are!" she said. "I would never go out with a person who takes such unnecessary chances with his life!" So much for the second date.

Now Ando was really getting confused and discouraged, but he persevered and in time, he got a third date. And you guessed it, they came to this same road crossing and the light was red again. Ando had tried two different ways previously and they both failed. This time, he decided to be smart and take a safer route. He gently asked his date while gazing at the red light, "What should we do now?" "SMACK!" Right across the face. Apparently, girls in Shanghai do this a lot! "What an imbecile you are!" she yelled at him. "Don't you know what to do when the light is red? I would never go out with a person as stupid as you!" Well, three strikes and you're out, although I don't know if this American baseball expression would apply in China. Poor Ando.

There is a moral to this story though. One can say that both timing and luck are important in life. Ando could have had three girlfriends instead of none if he had used the right approach at the right time. Alternatively, you can see a guy trying very hard to impress three different ladies and sadly, he failed to score each time because he couldn't figure them out in the right sequence. Then the moral is either men are really clueless when it comes to understanding women, or that women are not understandable in the first place and they will always remain a mystery to men! Your choice! My choice would be that Ando was simply unlucky in love! And it does take a bit of luck to find the right partner. So much for the joke.

Chapter 5

MY GREAT KOREAN ADVENTURE

Story #25

THE BEGINNING

It is strange sometimes how events in your life seem to line up and push you in a direction you hadn't intended to go. It is as if some unknown force was conspiring against you. I was enjoying my retirement, playing golf regularly with my golfing buddies. During one of these games, an ex-work colleague was invited to join us. His name is JC and he is Korean. It so happened that his long-time friend was the president of SK, a major engineering and construction company in Seoul, South Korea. The president was a visionary and because of his company's push towards globalization and business ventures outside South

Korea, he insisted that all staff in the Seoul office had to have an English first name because it was so difficult for foreigners to remember Korean names (which was true). While the female names like Shannon, Jenny and Sarah seemed quite normal, there have been some really unusual men's names like Maximillian, Rocky, Jesus, Augustino, Enoch and Brain. I think that the last one started out as Brian, but something got lost in the translation! Or maybe it was intentional as Brain was super intelligent!

Suncor had just awarded SK a major oilsands project for the design and construction on a complex secondary extraction process unit. This was the largest project ever outsourced for the Koreans to do in Canada. All the engineering design work was to be executed in Seoul. SK needed to open a Calgary subsidiary office in order to get the necessary Permit to Practise which would allow such foreign engineering designs to be accepted by APEGA (Association of Professional Engineers and Geoscientists of Alberta). They needed someone to set up and manage their engineering department and to recruit a team of Canadian professional engineers who would review all the Korean designs and authenticate their drawings. This was a huge responsibility as this team would essentially be held fully liable for all the technical work done by foreign engineers. If anything went wrong, the careers of these Canadian engineers would be finished.

There is a saying that *"to be lucky, you just have to be at the right place at the right time."* I was in the right place when JC needed a manager of engineering to fill this key role for this Calgary office, and I just happened to have held exactly such a position before I retired. The timing was right for me as I was making my wife unhappy the past couple of years by constantly "getting in her way" in my retirement. She wanted me to do something and get out of the house! I guess I didn't resist too much when I was asked to take on this critical role of engineering manager. This was also an opportunity for me to become a management consultant working for myself, something I had always wanted to do. However, I didn't want to work full time. I liked my retirement life. I told JC I didn't even want to work half time, but I was willing to give him a quarter of my time to help set up the office and to staff up the engineering team with people having the required expertise and experience. Within a year or two, if everything worked out and the project proceeded well, then I would go back to retirement. That was the plan, but what started out as a quarter time job, quickly became a half-time job, and for a short time more than a full-time job getting all the people in place and doing project work as well. What was just a concept that summer became a fully functional office of 20 people four months later. This company start-up was exciting and intense. It required a lot more work than anticipated. It was better suited for younger people, let alone two retired old guys like JC and I, being well past our physical prime! It was a good thing that we were still mentality on top of our game.

THE GERIATRIC GANG

I recruited a very diverse team of senior engineers. They were mainly the colleagues I had worked with and whose skills and technical knowledge I valued and trusted. They were the best engineers I knew, leaders in their respective engineering discipline because of their extensive expertise and experience. They were also old like me, either retired, semi-retired, or thinking of retirement. The average age of this team was about 67 years old! We did not intend to work a long time, and definitely not full time. I had expected that it would take two years to complete the engineering work, as we might not last that long! Our nickname, the "geriatric gang" was quite appropriate as it demonstrated that this bunch of old guys were not yet ready to be "put out to pasture!" We had plenty left to contribute and we knew that we could make a big difference to the success of the project.

It was an interesting adjustment period as this team of senior engineers, including myself, were somewhat set in our ways. We were not willing to compromise much on things we saw as being wrong or not good enough. I had to convince them that if the young engineers, no matter where they came from, were worthy of being mentored by each of us, then it was our duty to pass on our knowledge and experience to help the next generation. We would work as long as our contributions were making a positive difference to the project and that our efforts and expertise were recognized and appreciated. We had also planned to mentor qualified engineers, preferably Korean speaking, to replace us within the next two years. In all, I needed only 12 professional engineers across all the engineering disciplines to cover the review and validation of the calculations, designs and drawings done by the SK engineers for this mega-project! It is amazing what you can do when you have the right people who know how to do the right things all the time! I remembered a quote which said, "People are the most important asset." This was not entirely correct. "The right people are the most important asset!" I had the right group of engineers supporting the work of their Korean counterparts. Our collective experience and technical knowledge were second to none. Suncor acknowledged and appreciated SK for securing such a superior level of Canadian engineering expertise. It was pure luck that I had this golf game with JC and that I happened to be that "right" person he was seeking.

THE ENGINEERING DIFFERENCES

The Canadian engineers had to show the SK engineers what adjustments were needed in their designs to accommodate the cold weather conditions in northern Canada and how the facilities would be erected using a high degree of modularization. The bitterly cold winter months in northern Alberta made on-site construction very expensive. The SK engineers were used to designing for warm weather countries in south-east Asia and the Middle East where winter conditions were non-existent and construction could be done all year long. There were quite noticeable differences in how they did their engineering designs and plant layouts.

The front entrance lobby in the SK office tower in Seoul was two stories high. There was a photo mural on the wall adjacent to the main elevators. It showed the largest refinery complex built in South Korea by this company. It was a very impressive accomplishment reflective of the Korean superior engineering prowess. When I first saw this massive photo filling up the entire wall up to the ceiling, my gaze kept looking up and up and up. I asked myself, "Why was this facility designed so high?" and "Why were there so many pressure vessels and tanks installed up in the air supported by the steel structures instead of being installed on foundations on the ground the way they were done in Canada?" I learned later on that this was just the way they designed things because it was their cost effective and expedient method of designing. There was little integration or optimization between their structural steel and piping layout groups to reduce the amount of steel or piping used. If the steel structures were designed first, the pipe lines were just placed where the steel supports existed. If more supports were needed, they would just be added on. Changes needed in engineering to accommodate layout considerations were easily and quickly done. The cost for carbon steel piping and structural steel overseas was also lower as well as their costs for engineering. This made work done in South Korea to be very attractive from a cost reduction perspective. Suncor had selected the SK to do the engineering because of this cost advantage and their reputation for being able to meet schedules no matter what. While this might have been true for projects built in countries that did not have cold winter weather conditions, this was definitely not a cost effective way to do construction work in northern Alberta. Modular techniques had to be integrated into the designs to pack as much piping onto each pipe-rack module. This required more engineering to optimize both the modular steel pipe-rack structures and the layout of the equipment and piping on them.

This was an obvious difference in their plant layouts where their pipe-rack structures were set very high intentionally because it was so much easier to do. Initially, many of their pipe-rack structures were designed to be six stories high when the current norm for pipe-rack structures in Canada were three stories high maximum. I had the expertise in modular designs, having executed many projects designed and constructed with extensive modularization. Every time the SK engineers came up with equipment and piping layouts in high structures, I questioned why they needed to be so high. I had my Canadian engineers show them how to design modules that best met the shipping logistics and constraints and how the piping could be safely laid out and optimized. This was my greatest personal contribution to the project by defining and optimizing their modularization strategy. When I finally managed to reduce the height of all the pipe-rack structures down to a manageable three stories high, my team saved Suncor at least a couple hundred of million dollars in project costs avoidance. Something I doubted Suncor was aware of since this happened very early in the project and behind the scenes with the SK engineers. Even SK didn't initially realize how major a cost avoidance this was. This definitely helped them meet the project cost targets Suncor was expecting. It was a "win-win" all around simply because it was the right thing to do.

CHALLENGING SAID

The SK engineers on the project were very intelligent and well-educated. They were book-smart and they relied a lot on computers and technology for their designs and calculations. Based on the facilities they had successfully designed and built, they were proud of their accomplishments. They felt that they could compete, engineering-wise, with anyone in the world. This presented a dilemma for the Canadian engineers, especially Said, my senior civil/structural engineer. He was there to show them the nuances in designing for a cold climate country and why certain things had to be done the way he recommended. The SK engineers felt that they didn't need any Canadian engineer to tell them what to do. There was nothing Said could "teach" them. Being young and feeling invincible, this hubris came naturally to the SK engineers. I remembered the incident that changed this attitude.

Said was an "old guy" like me. He had over 30 years doing this type of complex civil and structural work. He was the best at what he did with extensive design and field experience, having "been there, seen that and done it all!" According to South Korean customs, old people were supposed to be respected because of their age. But this respect was never given to Said. His SK counterparts saw him as a competitor whose technical competency needed to be challenged. One day when Said was in the Seoul office for a couple of weeks interfacing with his SK engineers, they decided to present him with a structural design problem which they were having some difficulties solving. They gave him the drawings of the design problem in question, the computerized calculations and several text books they were using to try to solve the problem. Said started to look at the drawings as they were getting ready to leave. He said, "Where are you going?" They answered, "We thought you needed a couple of hours to review this problem and come back to us with the solution." "No need," said Said. "Here is your problem. Let me check your calculations." Sure enough, the computer calculations had a wrong input data entered which gave a result Said did not expect to see on the drawings.

Without looking at anything more, and not even opening any of the textbooks they provided him, he continued and said, "Here is the solution. Fix your calculations and do this change." He drew the design change right on the affected drawings he was reviewing. The SK engineers were dumbfounded. They just stood there with their mouths open. In the course of just 10 minutes, not only did Said find and confirm the problem, he immediately solved it. Of course, they checked Said's solution and without doubt, it was the right solution. Said must have encountered this same type of problem in his career and he knew exactly how to fix it immediately. Senior, experienced engineers had such insights. The SK engineers had a new found respect for and a better attitude towards Said. They started to listen to him and to see him as a positive influence in their work. They began to work as a team. Respect!

ELECTRIFYING SHARANA

Not all the SK engineers resisted the advice of the Canadian engineers. The way the electrical designs were completed was deemed to be an unparalleled success for the project in terms of cost effective and efficient designs. This was achieved with the exceptional cooperation between Sharana and Peter, the SK electrical lead engineer. Sharana was going to mentor Peter in the ways the electrical designs had to be done. They had to design and build complex electrical E-houses that were to be completely modularized with all the electrical equipment and control components fully integrated into these structures. The five E-houses were a major project by themselves as they would cost over $300 million to design and build.

Unlike the SK structural engineers who initially resisted Said's involvement and advice on their designs, Peter embraced Sharana's involvement from day one. He saw Sharana as a mentor with a wealth of knowledge and experience that he could learn from, something he would not find anywhere else. And he knew and appreciated that he was getting all this for free! Peter was already an accomplished and capable electrical engineer. He just lacked the experience Sharana had in being able to identify the potential problems and how these obstacles could be avoided by doing the right things early before the problems occurred. He was the ideal candidate worthy of Sharana's mentorship – someone who respected his expertise and who would listen and learn from him. Peter was that exceptional person and the project benefited immensely from this collaboration.

I asked Sharana how long he thought it would take for a smart person like Peter to "suck up" all the relevant knowledge he had accumulated over his entire career as an electrical engineer? He said simply, "About a month and a half!" This was so true. If I had to mentor someone in how to be an effective engineering manager and what were all the pitfalls to be avoided, it would probably take only a couple of months to do for the right person who really wanted to learn. Engineering designs and methods are not that complex once you know how they can be done right. It is just a question of knowing what you don't know and finding someone who has the solutions.

WORK AT THE SK TOWER

A typical day at work in the office would be like this. The Seoul office had about 2,000 people in one 22 stories high building. Most people would start work between 7-9 AM. When they got to their cubicles, they put their slippers on. Yes, they all wore slippers at work. This habit was so engrained that when several Koreans were working temporarily at the Calgary office, the first thing they asked for were slippers. The office had to send someone to the local Walmart to get them some! It was indeed a strange custom. Women dressed very smartly in Korea and they came to work fashionably dressed in short skirts which was the current fashion trend there. To maintain their decorum and modesty at work, they covered their laps with small pieces of cloth when they were sitting down. So prim and proper and polite. So Korean! The cubicles were all low, so everyone could see what everyone else was doing or saying. There was absolutely no privacy. Supervisors had bigger cubicles with higher partitions, but they were still open. The few offices they had were meant for the senior managers and executives. Just before 9 AM, the company theme song was played over the office intercom, followed by any company announcements in Korean and English, signifying the official start of the day. Thank goodness, they didn't do calisthenics. And then they worked, and did the SK staff ever work!

The Korean way of life appeared to be "work – work - and then work some more!" They seemed to have committed their lives to their company, generally working from 9 AM to 9 PM every day, except for Wednesday which was the designated "Family Night." One day a week, they could leave earlier at 6 PM! Unlike Canada with our TGIF (Thank God It's Friday!) mentality and everyone leaving early by 3 or 4 PM on Fridays, the SK personnel worked late even on the Fridays. The company provided subsidized breakfast, lunch <u>and</u> supper for all their staff. The top two floors in their tower were their full kitchen and dining facilities with menu options changing every day. There was no reason for anyone going home for dinner. If your supervisor worked late, it was improper, or it was looked down upon, if you left work before your boss did. But the supervisors never left early as that was how they became supervisors in the first place by working late every night. During the day at noon time, the lights would be turned off and it was common to see many of them, after a quick lunch, go back to their cubicles to take a short nap. At 1 PM the lights came back on, and everyone went back to work until the supper break at 6:30 – 7:30 PM. At about 9 PM, the supervisors left for home, and the rest of the staff could then leave too. Try this work day in our North American culture!

Furthermore, there was no overtime pay for these long hours of work. No wonder the productivity was so much higher in South Korea! They were so committed to their work! The typical employment contract was paid by the month and it had a clause which said something to the effect that the employee would do whatever was necessary to get their assigned work done - even if it took 12-16 hours every day of the week to do so! No one got overtime pay. The concept of hourly paid wages with overtime premiums was not the norm in South Korea. This topic even came up in the contract negotiations between the SK project director with the Suncor management because in Canada, it was against the law to make any overtime payments to a company that would not be given to the affected employees. This labour law had subsequently been changed to make overtime payments mandatory in South Korea. Such were the cultural differences that affected the working environment.

LIFE IN SEOUL

Seoul is an amazing city. It is very clean, safe, modern and vibrant, heavily populated with throngs of people everywhere and at all times of the day. There are 12 million people in the city core with about another 12 million in the outlying areas. This meant that for South Korea having a total population of about 50 million, almost half of them lived in and around Seoul.

South Korea reminded me of Japan in the early 1950-60's when the Japanese people were likewise fully committed to their companies and in dedicating their lives to build up their country's economy. I was very cautious not to compare the Koreans with the Japanese because of their bad historical experiences when Japan occupied Korea from 1910-1945. However, the parallels between the Japanese and Korean cultures were historically and politically intertwined. There were very few Japanese made cars in Seoul. Most cars were made in South Korea, like Kia and Hyundai. Speaking of Hyundai, I remembered distinctly a comedian's joke over 20 years ago when the Hyundai cars first came out in North America and the quality wasn't all that good initially. The punch line was "Hyundai is Korean for crap!" Well, that was a fairly insensitive and somewhat racist comment even if it were meant to be a joke. We can't say that now what with all these quality and innovative products coming from Samsung, LG and Hyundai. Made in South Korea products are challenging the domination of goods made in China and Japan. Hyundai actually means "modernity" or contemporary as in new thinking and new probabilities. This is an appropriate word for how South Korea has progressed. The main family-owned conglomerates, called chaebols, include Samsung. LG, Hyundai and the SK Group, have been the key drivers to the success of their economy and globalization. As a progressive country, South Korea is doing very well, and rightfully so, having achieved so much since their independence in 1945.

Working in Seoul had been a very enlightening experience as there were many cultural differences that North Americans wouldn't see until they have actually worked with them. All the Koreans looked young, slim and tall and generally good looking. Asians, in general, tended to look younger as if they were fresh out of high school in their early twenties. But in reality, they were more in their late thirties and even forties. In all the time I spent in Seoul, I saw only one fat person! There must have been more, and I was looking every day. This must have had something to do with their diet which was very healthy and lean with minimal deep-fried foods. Koreans considered Chinese foods to be very greasy compared with their basic rice, BBQ meats, noodles and soups, Kimchi (spicy pickled cabbage) and loads of vegetables. You also wouldn't see too many small children in the city, and when you did, they were usually from families outside of Seoul coming in over the weekend for a visit.

THE WIVES IN SEOUL

After a number of trips to Seoul by the Canadian engineering team, a number of us thought that it would be a good time for our wives to visit Seoul to see the sights while we were off working. On one of these two-week trips, four of our wives decided to join us in Seoul. We were all staying at the spacious Fraser Suites in the Insadong district, located near the tourist areas. This was an all-suites hotel with full kitchenette and separate bedroom. It was a very comfortable hotel located a mere 12 block walk to the office. Every morning the team would meet to have breakfast at the hotel dining room and then we would walk to the office to start work at 8 AM. Our wives came down after 8 AM for a more leisurely breakfast after all the men had left for work. We found out later, they would stay there until they closed the breakfast room at 10 AM. Then they went walking and shopping and sight-seeing at various places of interest. Later in the afternoon, they usually ended up at their favourite Parisienne Bakery Cafe where they had coffee or tea with delicious pastries. They did this _every_ day and they never tired of the routine as there was so much for them to do and to see. They got along remarkably well together. When the husbands finished work at 5 PM, unlike the SK engineers who worked late every night, we left to take our wives out for dinner, trying all the different foods and restaurants in the area. Seoul was quite a cosmopolitan city with a vast variety of international cuisines. Our wives were having a marvelous time and we were glad that they found ways to enjoy themselves while we were busy working. We never worried about them because Seoul was a very safe city anywhere and the people were so polite.

ML, the SK project director, did a very unexpected thing. He knew our wives were with us and he invited them to join us for dinner one evening at the company's private dining room up in the corner of their cafeteria. Normally when they were entertaining existing or new clients who wished to see their office facilities, they would be treated to either lunch or dinner prepared by their corporate chefs. They never included any wives as this was not the custom in South Korea for wives to be involved in any part of their husbands' businesses. In North America, it was quite normal for wives to regularly be part of the company's corporate and client functions and in getting to know the other wives. In South Korea, business functions were done by the men, usually going some place to eat copiously and drinking lots of soju, the Korean rice wine. I suspected ML knew of this cultural difference. This was nevertheless a new and very different experience for all of us.

The wives were interested in a tour of the office as they heard, no doubt from us, how hard the SK people worked. They were also curious to see what we actually did when we went to work every morning. When they arrived at the SK Tower, we gave them a quick tour of the office. Then ML showed up and he accompanied us to the top floor where the corporate private dining room was located. It was already supper time and the people dining there looked at our group curiously as they had never seen so many foreign couples walking together going to dinner. We must had been quite a sight with our diverse mix of nationalities. My wife, Pat, and I would fit in because we were Chinese, Sharana and his wife, Ratna, were East Indian, Fraser and his better half, Helen, were Scottish and Said and his wife, Aspasia, were Egyptian/Greek. The group certainly met the melting pot image of Canada. ML had invited a few of our engineering counterparts to join us, but none of their Korean wives were there. He was a very gracious host making sure that he paid attention to each of our wives and he made them feel comfortable. The food selection was distinctively Korean, so most of us didn't know exactly what we were eating. It was nevertheless delicious and delightful. Our wives have fondly remembered this special dinner and how the SK management were so welcoming and considerate.

DINING WITH THE LOCALS

My colleague, Kee, who helped me show the SK engineers how to do modular pipe-racks, was a "foodie." He liked trying out the foods the locals ate, especially foods sold in the streets. He introduced me and Wayne, who did the piping modular designs, to the very tasty experience of eating grilled mackerel fish at his favourite street vendor frequented by him many times in the district where only local Koreans ate. Tourists rarely ventured into this area. As we were walking there, we passed by an interesting place that looked like a restaurant as many local people were going in and out. The counter at the window displayed all sorts of tempting fresh seafoods. The daily catch included razor clams, varying types of whole fish, shrimps with their heads intact, scampi, clams, snails, octopus and scallops. "Let's try this place one day," we said to each other, nodding approvingly.

Well, that day came and for some reason we were dressed in our business suits and ties, looking very much like business men carrying briefcases. Now this "restaurant" was really the proverbial "hole-in-the-wall" place, and it was very spartan. It was run by a husband-and-wife team that did the cooking and cleaning, waiting on the tables, cashier and host. Only locals went there to eat as the food was very good and not expensive. The locals were definitely not dressed like us. It was not a conventional restaurant with regular chairs and tables. In their place, people sat on small plastic crates over short wooden box-like tables. The ceiling in the eating area was only six feet high, so people had to crouch down to get into the place! Imagine this scene. The three of us entered the shop and the owners looked up with a bit of surprise, seeing three smartly dressed Asian guys standing there. I could see in their facial expression, "What are you doing here?!" They knew that we were Chinese as Kee and Wayne frequently spoke in their own dialect when they were together. As we didn't speak their language, other than the perfunctory "an-nyeong-ha-se-yo" (hello/goodbye) and "kam-sa-ham-ni-da" (thank-you), we flashed three fingers for a table for three!

The owner boss immediately took charge and escorted us to an oversized wooden box that served as a table with three plastic crate boxes for chairs. Very classy! We had to crouch down to get into the low ceiling area. The other dozen or so diners already crammed in the room looked at us curiously as we settled in. We made eye contact with a few of them by nodding and saying hello to them. They returned our greeting and smiled back. Koreans were so polite and welcoming. Kee went to the counter and in universal sign language, he pointed at all the things we liked to try eating and then he pointed to either the grill or the steaming pot of hot water. We were cautious not to eat raw seafood, so the fish was grilled and everything else was blanched. We ordered two types of grilled fish, fresh shrimps, razor clams and octopus tentacles. Rice came with the seafood which was brought piping hot to our table. Kee ordered two bottles each of soju and Cass beer which we enjoyed with our dinner. We were eating the same way the locals were. It was one of the best meals we had ate in Seoul. The seafood couldn't have been any fresher.

When we finished, Kee got up and he went to the front to pay. He took out all his Korean currency and the wife owner simply took whatever she thought was right. Koreans were also very honest! He gave her the thumbs up while rubbing his stomach to show our appreciation of their cooking. The bill came to a whopping 38,000 Korean wons, or $42 Cdn! What a deal! When we got ready to leave, still crouching under the low ceiling, the other seated diners waved us goodbye and the owners bowed to us and we did also in return. I thought that they would remember this time when unexpected well-dressed tourists patronized their little place and enjoyed their cooking. Most people would consider his restaurant to be a "dump", even to the locals. Now it had "class!" No doubt, we would always remember this welcoming little place for both its delicious seafoods and its unique ambiance and humble hospitality that made it so special.

One final observation about cooking. We noticed that all the cooks were middle-aged or older women. Young Korean women do not know how to cook! Just ask anyone in Seoul. Like our generation of millennials, young women would just order out for food as opposed to learning how to cook it for themselves.

THE ALLURING LADIES OF SEOUL

I have always been fairly observant of the opposite sex, especially when it came to which country had the most attractive women. In St. Peterburg, Russia, the women were tall, blond and statuesque, like the tennis player, Maria Sharapova. In Paris, France, the women were sophisticated, fashionable and tres chic. I liked the women in Barcelona, Spain, for their dark and sultry Mediterranean looks. Then there were these alluring ladies of Seoul who were youthful looking, slim, fit and very shapely with the classical Asian features. Seoul is world renowned for its extensive use of plastic surgery which at least half of their women have used to enhance various parts of their faces and bodies. Women, who know that they are good-looking, dress and act accordingly to accentuate their attractiveness. This is just a natural law of the sexes. When you got it, you can certainly flaunt it! And men have no choice but to look at and admire such beauties! My pre-dominantly all-male engineering team was no exception.

One evening, a few of us were enjoying crispy chicken wings with Cass beer at our favourite restaurant. Yes, Seoul had their own version of KFC (Korean fried chicken) which was much less greasy than the traditional fare from Colonel Saunders. My colleague, Dale, kept looking up and staring in one direction, seemingly fixated on something. "What are you looking at?" I asked. "That woman … I'm going to marry her!" he mumbled. "What are you talking about? You are already happily married!" I looked in the direction he was staring and I could see this very nice-looking Korean girl. Dale was enamoured by her oriental beauty. I was more immune to her spell since I already have a beautiful wife. "Your wife wouldn't like you staring at strange women hoping to marry them!" I said. I remembered his response, "Well, I am not dead! And I am only looking!" He has since compared every other Asian woman to this dream Korean woman.

Dale was not the only one bewitched by the women in Seoul. Normally, all the engineering team members stayed at the Fraser Suites because of the kitchen facilities and separate bedroom. One time, both Kee and Wayne decided to stay at another hotel, the Royal Park, which was closer to the office location. This was just a standard hotel, so I dropped by after work just to see why they wanted to go there. The hotel was located right on one of the main shopping streets in Seoul, and there were always throngs of people, both local and tourists, milling about. If you liked hustle and bustle, this was the place for action. When I arrived at the hotel, Kee and Wayne were already outside the hotel, leaning against the front entrance patio. "What are you doing?" I asked. "Looking at the women," they replied. I looked up and I could see why. There was this continuous stream of good-looking Asian women, fashionably dressed in very short skirts walking by. That's what they did every evening after work and dinner. Instead of watching boring TV in their small hotel room, they entertained themselves looking at the women. As both were also happily married, like Dale, I surmised that they were only just looking as well and admiring the beauty all around them! Men! So predictable!

I, too, wasn't immune to these alluring ladies of Seoul. One day while walking the usual 12 blocks to the office, I encountered a shapely lady who was walking just ahead of me. She had these long lovely legs and a backside that moved provocatively with each step she took. She knew she was good-looking and she dressed accordingly in a very short skirt and fashionable high heel shoes that accentuated her bare and tanned legs. It certainly caught my attention and this vision of her walking so seductively was mesmerizing. So much so, I followed her discreetly for a good six blocks! I didn't want to pass her to get a good look of her face as I was afraid that this might destroy my vision of this absolute perfection of a woman from the backside! My wife knew that I had this roving eye. But I guessed that as long as I was just looking and did nothing more than using my excuse that I was admiring beauty in all forms, then it would be tolerated. What a fortunate guy I was to have such an understanding wife!

THE ENDING

Initially, I had a fairly difficult time integrating and understanding the Korean way of work. I was used to giving orders and I had a hard time taking orders and advice from others. I tended to question many of their decisions especially when they didn't make sense to me. When they didn't answer me and seemingly ignored my questions, I used to take this personally until I found out that they simply didn't know how to respond to my direct and aggressive North American manner. This made the SK project director upset many times because I was not doing things the Korean way even though he knew that I was a Chinese who grew up and was educated in Canada. As a result, my attitudes and thinking were much more Westernized. In their culture, they didn't value individual excellence or initiative, or people questioning the things their superiors did especially when they were considered to be subordinates. The main thing they valued most was conformance – which in South Korea, meant following orders without question. I was like a fish out of water. I simply couldn't quite fit in.

The end of my association with the Korean Calgary company occurred after three years. My contract was terminated by them for essentially me being too difficult a person to work with even though this was never the stated reason. They wanted to control me in all aspects, but I would not let them do things which I felt were not right to do. I've always been this way and I am still very black and white on matters of engineering and public safety. I would not take, nor allow, any short cuts to be taken that would have compromised the safety of the engineering work, just to meet their schedules. Our cultural and professional differences eventually became irreconcilable. The contract I had signed with SK could be terminated by a written notice from either party, and without need for any reason or justification to be stated. This clause was initially included in case we couldn't work together. Yet we managed to work together for three years despite our differences. At the end, I did my best to ensure that this major Suncor project would be properly designed and engineered. I finally ended up doing it the Korean way by quietly leaving and not complaining to Suncor when my contract was eventually ended. It would have been unethical of me to have said any negative things about the company who gave me the opportunity to be a key part in the success of such a significant project. It had been the largest engineering project I had ever managed and executed.

The $17 billion Suncor Fort Hills Project successfully started up in 2017 and everything worked as designed. Today, it meets its 194,000 barrels per day production capacity. The $4 billion portion of the Secondary Extraction Plant had the distinction of being the largest process unit ever awarded to a foreign company who essentially did all the engineering outside of Alberta. How did the SK engineers do? Suncor's feedback was simple and direct: "Engineering and Procurement were outstanding. Modularization was deemed to be good." Outstanding engineering? Not bad at all! It was a fitting conclusion and an excellent way to end my engineering career with "My Great Korean Adventure."

Chapter 6

IN SEARCH OF ALEXANDRITE

<u>Story #26</u>

HOW IT ALL STARTED

In 1972, the year after I had graduated from McGill University with a Mechanical Engineering degree and after securing a full-time job, I proposed to Pat, my wife-to-be. A friend of the family in Hong Kong had purchased this gorgeous emerald cut solitaire diamond engagement ring for me. This ring was set in 18 kt white gold and I got it for a really good price because the diamond was supposedly just under one carat. I paid only $600 which was the equivalent of just a month's salary. One might say that I was a really cheap guy as the normal expectation was to spend two to three months salary for an engagement ring that would make a lasting impression. The ring was simple and elegant. It certainly didn't look cheap! Besides, it was all I could afford at that time, having just started my engineering career.

Good thing I remembered that she preferred emerald cut gems over the traditional round brilliant cut diamonds used in most engagement rings. This ring was not appraised until 16 years later. To us, it was just an engagement ring, and a relatively cheap one based on the price I had paid. We didn't think too much about gemstones in our early years of marriage as our time was consumed with work, raising a family and buying a car and a house – all much more important than spending money on frivolous things like jewellery. Like all things in life, this was about to change.

On a family vacation to see the sights of Southern California, my wife and our two young sons were in San Diego walking around in the Gastown district. We were walking by a jewellery store when their window display beckoned us to stop and look. It was filled with all sorts of jewellery and gemstones that glittered in all the colours of the rainbow. We didn't know what type of gemstones they were, only that we liked the red coloured ones. After all, red is the favoured colour for the Chinese as it denotes joy, good luck and happiness.

A salesman inside saw us looking at the window and he came out and invited us in to browse around. I told him that we were on vacation and just looking and not really interested in buying anything. However, we did go in because we wanted to see what else they had. It must have been a quiet morning that day as there was only another elderly couple inside. We were looking around their display counters while our two boys found ways to keep themselves occupied outside near the front door. The manager of the store appeared with a small jewellery box in his hand. He opened it and showed whatever was in the box to the elderly couple. He seemed very pleased with himself. Looking up and seeing that we were the only other people in his store, he asked my wife:

"Please come over and have a look at this beautiful ring I designed and made for them."

He wanted to see what my wife's first impression would be of his custom designed ring. He was obviously very proud of the workmanship. It was a lady's ring with a huge brilliant-cut diamond at least 5 carats in size. It was humungous. The center diamond was surrounded by not the small speck-like "diamond dust" diamonds commonly used to add "bling" to inexpensive rings. Instead, full-sized diamonds at least 1/3rd carats each were used and there were at least 10 of them surrounding the main gem! This was one impressive and expensive ring, dazzling so brightly in the store lighting. The elderly couple must have had loads of money to burn to have such a huge ring custom made for them.

My wife took one look at the ring on the elderly lady's finger and she blurted out loudly, "It's blinding!" The manager must have heard all the adjectives to describe diamonds, but he had yet to hear this "blinding" word, and he liked it. "Exactly!" he responded. He was very pleased with the spontaneous reaction from my wife. The elderly couple exchanged appreciative nods, satisfied that their new ring could make such a striking first impression, even from a stranger!

As we browsed around, my wife was drawn to a big, red ring that was beautifully displayed in a locked cabinet. None of the gemstones we saw at the window could compare with the dazzle and deep red colour of this ring. The manager noted her interest and he walked over. As he unlocked the case, he said to my wife, "You have a very keen eye for gemstones. This is one of my best rings." He was more than happy to take it out and show it to her. I guess he really liked my wife and her spontaneous reaction to the diamond ring. He proceeded to tell us more. The gemstone was a rare Burmese ruby with the classic and most sought-after "pigeon-blood" red colour. The ruby was quite large, just about 3 carats, and it was a brilliant-cut gemstone with smaller diamonds all around it. The ruby gem was the star and the sparkle of the whole ring was intense and eye-catching. The manager continued, "The sparkle of this ruby is very nice inside, but wait until you see it outside." He then invited my wife to put the ring on her finger and go out and look at the gemstone in the direct sunlight. This was the first time my wife experienced a security guard accompanying her outside. While the ruby was already impressive in its fiery sparkle inside the store, the fire and brilliance of this sparkle was twice as strong in the sunlight. The red colour was so vivid and intense. It was the most beautiful red we had ever seen! All my wife could say was "WOW!" It was only years later when we learned more about coloured gemstones, we realized that this was indeed an extremely rare ruby from Burma (now Myanmar). Only Burmese rubies would tend to fluoresce so strongly and noticeably in the sunlight. We had seen one of the very best! And my wife had the pleasure of wearing this ruby ring, even if it were for just a few minutes. We thanked the manager for his time and for showing us his prized ruby ring. He thanked us, or specifically my wife, for making his day.

Incidentally, that ring was very expensive selling for $12,000 US! To put this price into context, at that time I was driving a Mazda GLC which I had purchased new at $6,000 Cdn. I could have easily bought two cars at the price of this exceptional ruby ring! Today, if you could even find a Burmese ruby gemstone of this colour and size for sale, you would probably pay at least $300,000 for the ring! Most of the best Burmese rubies are in museums or in private collections. In hindsight, I should have bought it, despite whether I had the money or not! But that's life. I was not cheap, just realistically poor! Sometimes, you don't know what treasures you could have had until they are gone! Who knew then that rare and quality gemstones like this ruby could appreciate so much in value. It certainly changed our views of how financially rewarding gemstone collecting can be.

ESSENTIALS OF GEMSTONE COLLECTING

When we got back home, gemstones were definitely on our minds. Now I wanted to get my wife's engagement ring appraised. But first, I had to find a gemologist. We were very fortunate in finding a reputable gemologist who was quite a character. I remember him fondly, Barry D. Blower from Edmonton. He was quite a fastidious man who looked like a hippie because he wore a pony tail and he would wash his hands constantly when performing an appraisal. Formerly trained as a goldsmith at Birks Jewellery in Montreal, he was also an opera singer before becoming a really good and qualified GIA (Gemological Institute of America) gemologist! Talk about diverse occupations! He was very conservative and absolutely precise in his appraisals. He even served as the jewellery expert whenever the police agencies needed him at court. He was perfect to do our first appraisal.

Because the diamond was still set in its ring, it was difficult for him to confirm its exact carat size. Barry did a couple of external measurements using different tools and one result showed the diamond to be just under a carat and the other one just over.

"Why does it matter?" I asked. He responded, "It makes a big difference in its appraised value whether it is over or under 1 carat. I think it will be worthwhile to take the diamond out of its setting, weigh it and find out for sure."

Since he was also a goldsmith, he could easily remove and re-set the gemstone. I agreed. It weighed exactly 1.000 carat! This was an unexpected result as I always believed that the diamond was less than a carat in size based on the bargain price I had paid for it. It was one full carat precisely. This diamond should have sold for a much higher price than the measly $600 I initially paid. Premiums at 25 to 100% are expected to be paid for quality gemstones whenever they are precisely at or over each size category of 1, 2 and 3 carats. Don't ask me why. This is just a peculiarity in the gemstone industry. You can't see the difference from a 0.999 carat gem to one that is exactly 1.000 carat and explain why the latter can be worth so much more than the marginally smaller one, everything else being equal. The pleasant surprise came when he appraised this engagement ring at over $12,000! This was 20 times higher than what I had paid for it! I could no longer be considered cheap! Just lucky.

Barry gave us the best advice on how to collect gemstones and jewellery. "Buy what you like and what you can afford," he told us, "and always try to get gemstones that are both natural and untreated." It is easy to collect jewellery when you are rich and money is not a limitation. Not everyone can be like the elderly couple in San Diego who could easily afford to pay whatever the price may be for any expensive item they wanted. It is much harder when you want to create value by buying gemstones on a budget and making your own unique jewellery designs.

Besides being a gemologist, Barry maintained a side business as a goldsmith making and selling custom jewellery. He sold us our first coloured gemstone, a natural and untreated 1.9 carat Ceylon blue sapphire. Then he made the custom ring for my wife. We were following his advice. Because natural and untreated gemstones are so rare and difficult to find these days, they will always appreciate in value over time, doubling and tripling and even more. When you are so fortunate to even find some, you will have to decide whether you can afford the asking price. The natural and untreated gemstones in our collection are modest in size, but they are still special enough to be considered family heirlooms. The early advice on collecting gemstones was great, but luck was also a big contributing factor in finding quality gemstones at a reasonable price. We have purchased jewellery and gemstones from many sources – auction houses, newspaper ads, gemologists, goldsmiths and established jewellery stores. We couldn't have done this with any confidence without knowing a qualified gemologist who would validate our purchases from whatever source.

The next person you need is a really good goldsmith who can turn the gemstones into unique custom-designed jewellery you would be proud to own and wear. When we moved to Calgary, we were fortunate to find such an exceptionally skilled goldsmith whom we have known now for over 30 years. His name is Peter Jost and he was classically trained in Germany as a master craftsman. He is semi-retired now although his place of work, "The Goldschmiede Studio", is still active as is his website www.peterjost.ca. He uses the "goldschmiede" spelling of goldsmith as it is more sophisticated and reflective of his "old school" skills and traditions. The distinctive jewellery he had designed and made for us over the years had always been more like works of art than just mere pieces of jewellery. Unlike other jewellery establishments that may focus primarily on maximizing their profits, Peter was more interested in doing his best work artistically. I guess Peter liked making the unique custom jewellery for us because I always valued and appreciated his creativity. I liked his very "quirky" sense of humour. I think he liked the challenges I gave him trying to convert my rough sketches into workable designs. I may be the only one who insists on him signing every piece of jewellery he made for us as if all his artistic works were his masterpieces which they are indeed! He said that we have become "best" friends over the years.

We are all generally familiar with diamonds as almost everyone has one, but what about the coloured gemstones? The traditional coloured gemstones that have been widely sought after are the classic red rubies, blue sapphires and green emeralds. Of course, there are other gemstones that may be equally beautiful and worth collecting, but these do not have the historical significance or cachet of the classical three, making these gemstones solid investment potentials. Over the years, we have acquired many diverse gemstones and turned them into unique one-of-a-kind jewellery. We have collected diamonds, emeralds, sapphires and rubies as well as some of the less known gemstones such as opals, black pearls, jade, ammolite and amethyst for their beautiful colours.

Then there are those very unique gemstones which display different colours under varying lighting and viewing conditions, literally changing colour right before your eyes. It is quite amazing to see this colour transition. The most famous of such colour-changing gemstones is alexandrite because of its deep historical significance and reputation. Very few people know about it, and fewer have even seen this unusual and rare gemstone. The search for alexandrite proved to be the most elusive and challenging to find.

WHAT IS ALEXANDRITE?

Alexandrite is a rare variety of chrysoberyl which exhibits a distinct colour change under different lighting conditions. It is a pleochroic (colour changing) gemstone – ideally being a blue-green gemstone in natural daylight and changing to a rich ruby red or deep red-purple under incandescent lights. The best alexandrite gems have a medium tone and intense, near vivid colour and a very distinct and full colour transition. In terms of hardness, diamonds are the hardest, followed by the sapphires in the corundum family. Then comes alexandrite. Sapphires come in many colours, but they are best known for their blue colour. Red-coloured sapphires are called rubies and there are pink sapphires and other colours. The green emeralds belong to the beryl family of gemstones and they are not as hard as the diamond, sapphire and alexandrite. All these classic gemstones are worth collecting.

Originally discovered in the Ural Mountains of Russia in 1840, alexandrite was made famous by the Russian monarchy because red and green represented the principal colours of Imperial Russia. It was named after Czar Alexander II. Some also call this the "Christmas" gemstone. These initial gemstones from Russia have long since been mined out over the last 100 years. The uniqueness and rarity of alexandrite were made popular in America in the 1800's, specifically at Tiffany's, as the most famous and expensive chrysoberyl variety – a reputation it continues to hold to date. True Russian alexandrite gemstones, if you can find them, will sell for twice or three times their equivalents from other sources. Like the Burmese rubies with similar historical prestige and scarcity, most of their best gemstones are in museums or estate collections.

The discovery of fine Brazilian alexandrite in 1987 in the Hematita region reset that standard. The unique colour change from red to green comes from traces of chromium. While the Russian gemstones display a better green in daylight, many experts agree that the purple-reds (raspberry) of the Brazilian stones are clearly superior. By 2014 this Brazilian source also became depleted, just like what happened to the original Russian alexandrite. There are other limited sources of fine alexandrite available from India, Tanzania, Burma (Myanmar), Sri Lanka and Madagascar, but generally, their quality and colours are less than the ones from Russian and Brazil.

Alexandrite became the holy grail of my gemstone collection. I definitely wanted a gemstone that could change colours like this. It would be so special to own one. This turned out to be one of the more difficult of gemstones to find, especially in any size over 1 carat. No doubt, alexandrite will maintain its value and appreciate over time. As a result, top quality alexandrite is hardly ever available and it is never used in mass-marketed jewellery. It is simply too expensive for the general public to buy.

Alexandrite was the original birthstone for anyone born in June. I was born in June. That is why I wanted one for myself, and not for my poor wife whose birthstone is the common diamond. Because alexandrite was so rare and hard to get, the June birthstone had to be changed to something more available and affordable, like pearl. There is absolutely no comparison between alexandrite and pearl! What a drastic demotion of the original June birthstone!

FINDING ALEXANDRITE

In 2013, we were on a family cruise with our grandchildren on the Disney ship Fantasy cruising the Caribbean islands. One of the ports of call was in Philipsburg in St. Maarten. Typical of every cruise line, they would highlight the sights to be seen at each port and the best places for local shopping, especially jewellery stores. Something caught our eyes when Disney advertised that one of their recommended jewellery shops had the best collection of alexandrite gemstones ever in their Mark Henry Collection. It had been 15 years of fruitless searching for any quality alexandrite. Wherever we travelled overseas, we had always tried to stop by local jewellery shops where I would ask to see if they had any alexandrite jewellery. Most shops didn't even know what this rare gemstone looked like. Those shops who claimed to have alexandrite would only come up with disappointingly small gemstones in the ¼ to 1/3 carat sizes which were so muted in their colours that they didn't demonstrate any colour change. So, I wasn't expecting too much when my wife and I disembark at St. Maarten. The rest of our family had more fun going to the beach while we went shopping.

There were many jewellery stores on the main street in Philipsburg, and each shop had someone at its entrance beckoning us to enter to see their goods. But we were focused on going directly to Majesty Jewelers who supposedly were the only store that had all the quality alexandrite jewellery. A word of caution here in buying gemstones from any random jewellery store. While we might go in to have a look at what's available, we were cautious not to buy anything of significance from local independent stores, especially in a foreign country. You don't know what you might get as there are many fake and synthetic gemstones and unscrupulous shops who would sell inferior or counterfeit goods to unsuspecting tourists. Even shops that offered written appraisals are suspect as these documents could be easily doctored to over-inflate the appraised values in order to get people to pay more than what the jewellery was worth. In the case of Majesty Jewelers, we were not overly concerned as they were the jewellery shop recommended by the Disney Cruise Line. Shops had to be ethical and really good in their services and products in order to be promoted by such a reputable and prestigious organization like Disney. In other words, we trusted Disney!

The shop was quite large, modern and brightly lit with jewellery and watches all separated by categories in various areas of the store. It was bustling with tourists shopping for bargains during the late afternoon. We were greeted by a salesperson inside who directed us to the counter where the Mark Henry Collection of jewellery was displayed. She said that Jay, the store manager, would speak to us personally since people interested in alexandrite were definitely not bargain hunters. Coincidently, Marissa, the shopping director for the Disney cruise ship, happened to be in the store. I guessed she was also interested in seeing these amazing alexandrite gemstones. She listened in while I spoke to Jay.

"I hear you have some really good quality alexandrite gemstones?" I asked. "I've been looking for a very long time."

"Yes", Jay said, nodding with confidence. "They recently found a new source of alexandrite gemstones in Brazil and we have some of the best gemstones set in rings in the Mark Henry Collection." He pointed to the sparkling rings in the adjacent cabinet.

What I saw blew my mind. There were five lady's rings which stood out prominently. Each was designed to accentuate an alexandrite gemstone over 1 carat in size! In all the years of searching, I had never seen any alexandrite over ½ carat in size and none worth considering. And now, there was not one, but five rings with the biggest alexandrite gems I had ever seen! They were all dazzling red under the bright halogen lights in the store. Jay could see that I was duly impressed.

"These are quite nice rings, and big too!" I said, trying hard not to show my excitement. I made a mental note of the fairly expensive cost of each ring ranging between $20,000 to $30,000 US. Jay then took out an ultraviolet flashlight to confirm that the gemstones were true alexandrite by showing the distinctive red to green colour transition that was their defining characteristic.

The colour change was quite visible from red to green under the ultraviolet light. I remarked, "The colour change looks good under this artificial lighting, but what is the colour change really like in natural daylight?"

Jay looked at me and said nonchalantly, "Why don't I put these five rings on your wife's fingers and we can look at all of them outside and compare their colour change in the sunlight?"

Huh? We can do that? My wife put all these expensive rings on her fingers of her left hand and with a burly security guard accompanying us, we went outside. This was the second time my wife had been escorted out by an armed security guard! I will always remember this incident because it was something surreal that will never, ever happen again. We were standing outside, just in front of the store entrance – my wife, Jay, his security guard and Marissa, all looking at my wife's left hand wearing the five rings. I estimated they were worth well over $130,000 US! The sunlight was strong and there were no clouds in the sky. The street was filled with tourists milling about and they casually glanced at my wife's hand held up in the sunlight as they walked by. The colour change was immediate as the gemstones turned from the red-purple colour inside the store to varying shades of pale green and green-blue outside in the direct sunlight. Remarkable! Of the five rings, one of them, the alexandrite gemstone that was emerald cut, had the most pronounced and complete colour change. My wife liked it the best, and maybe because it was the only ring with her favoured emerald cut gemstone.

My wife has this uncanny knack that when given several things to choose from, she will always invariably pick the best and most expensive one. I like to think that she chose me because I'm the best, even though I may be cheap! Jay concurred that the ring my wife chose indeed had the best alexandrite gemstone. The ring was quite nicely designed, set in 18 kt white gold with two matching 0.3 carat trillium cut diamonds. The alexandrite gemstone at 1.03 carat was definitely over the 1 carat mark where a price premium would be expected to be paid. The ring had an appraisal value of $29,700 US, but it was selling at a reduced price of only $28,300 US! This was still very close to full retail. It was getting hot in the afternoon sun, so we all walked back inside to the air-conditioned store. Jay put the rings back securely in their locked display cabinet.

I said to Jay, "We have a problem here because I am not buying this ring for my wife."

Jay looked at me somewhat perplexed. He thought the ring was for my wife since she chose it. He looked at her with an expression sort of mentally saying to her, "Your husband doesn't think you are worth this ring?"

My wife just gave him a small smile and said, "My husband has been looking for an alexandrite ring for himself for quite a while as alexandrite is his birthstone, not mine."

I confirmed to Jay, "This gemstone is for me and I don't need the lady's ring setting. Would you consider selling me just the gemstone? And if so, how much?"

Jay knew that the alexandrite gem was the star of each ring and that any ring setting could be re-used by simply finding another dimensionally equivalent cut gemstone to be re-set in its place. Business being business, a sale of this dollar magnitude could not be ignored. Jay thought for a brief moment and he replied. "How about $23,000?" He had deducted $5,300 for the ring setting with the diamonds. I frowned and I countered with $20,000. I had never expected to pay so much for just a loose gemstone and definitely not while I was on a family vacation! I had no idea whether this was a fair price or that I was excessively overpaying. All I knew was that I had been searching unsuccessfully for many years and if I didn't buy this gemstone that day, even at a bloody full-blown retail price, I might never find another one! Marissa and my wife were watching intently as we negotiated the price. We were so serious staring at each other. Jay frowned back at me and he countered with $22,000. I gave my final "take it or leave it" price at $21,000, preparing to walk away. Well as they say, a sale is better than no sale. It was accepted! The negotiation sure ended quicker than expected. I think Marissa was surprised that anyone would pay such a high amount for a loose gemstone that wasn't even set in a ring!

The good thing about free enterprise is that a purchase deal occurs only when both seller and buyer feel they are getting the best price they can get for it. So, I guess what I paid did reflect the current market value at that time. I had to use two credit cards to pay for this gemstone. Jay then took me to his nondescript goldsmith shop a couple of blocks down the street. He had his goldsmith remove the gemstone, put this $21,000 US purchase into a little plastic pouch no bigger than two-inch square, and he unceremoniously gave it to me. That was it! No fancy jewellery box, no special carrying bag. No formal appraisal of the gemstone! Nothing. So much for any elaborate gift wrapping! Talk about cheap! But I was glad my long search for the elusive "holy grail" alexandrite had ended.

THE APPRAISAL

When I got back to the cruise ship with my precious possession, I immediately sent an email to the Disney corporate office in Miami and copied to Jay at Majesty Jewelers. This was to advise them in writing that when I got home, I was going to have the gemstone appraised locally to confirm that it was indeed a natural Brazilian alexandrite with superior colour-changing characteristics. I would advise them of the results. This was my insurance policy to get back, with Disney's help, any monies paid to Majesty Jewelers if this gemstone proved to be a fake.

In Calgary, there weren't too many gemologists with the necessary GIA (Gemological Institute of America) accreditation who also specialized in the appraisal of coloured gemstones. Most gemologists are very competent in grading diamonds, but their experience may vary for coloured gemstones as there are so many different types. Jack and Ron Hanania are brothers at IGL Laboratories, an established and reputable appraisal company in the city. They knew all the coloured gemstones, but I was not sure if they ever personally handled or examined an investment grade alexandrite gemstone over 1 carat in size. I called them to see if they were interested in doing an appraisal. They probably knew about this recent new recent source of quality Brazilian alexandrite, but they hadn't seen any yet. Silly question. Of course, they were interested!

Jack, the older brother, did the appraisal evaluation. The gemstone was completely red in the incandescent lighting in his office. After telling the story of how I purchased the gemstone while on vacation and the high retail price I had to pay for it, he immediately weighed the loose gemstone and he confirmed that it was indeed 1.03 carats. This put the gemstone in the investment grade category. Then he put the red alexandrite under ultra-violet lights and, sure enough, the gemstone turned completely to green. So far, so good. Then he inspected it very thoroughly under his microscope.

"Hmmm," he said, looking somewhat perplexed.

"What does this hmmm mean?" I asked. Now I was also a bit concerned.

He continued, "This gemstone is too clean."

I knew exactly what he meant. Usually, all gemstones have inclusions or other trace elements which would determine the origin of its source and whether they are natural or have been altered or heat-treated. For example, most emeralds have inclusions, but the characteristics of these inclusions help identify whether they were the desired emeralds from Columbia. When absolutely no inclusions are seen, the gemstones can be man-made as only clean base materials would have been used to make the fakes. Synthetic alexandrite imitations have been available in the past 100 years, made from corundum (a sapphire material) laced with trace elements like chromium to achieve the colour change. Natural inclusions help identify the source of the gemstone and differentiates it from lab-grown synthetic ones.

"But wait," he said. "Let me check it out further with some other instruments." He went into the adjoining room to test it for properties of wavelength, refractive index and specific gravity. What seemed to be a long time, he returned, looking somewhat pleased.

"Congratulations. I have good news." He said, "This alexandrite is from Brazil and it is real, natural and untreated." He elaborated further, "This gemstone is unusually clear with no inclusions whatsoever." Typically, even the highest graded clarity for alexandrite would still have some inclusions. This one had none which made it even more rare. It was akin to finding a flawless diamond or a Columbian emerald that was eye-clean.

Wow! I certainly lucked out. Then the next step was to determine what the appraised value should be despite the $21,000 US I had paid for it. Jack checked various gemstone pricing publications, including the major gem industry wholesalers in Canada and the USA, to see what alexandrite gemstones may have been sold recently. There were none of this size or shape to compare with. Even with this new source of quality alexandrite from Brazil, there was not enough pricing data to set its current market value. So, he set the appraisal of the gemstone at a low conservative value of $20,500 Cdn. I accepted this lower figure as I knew that this gemstone would appreciate greatly once the source at the Brazilian mines became depleted. This would be similar to what happened with original alexandrite from Russian. Besides, the appraisal value was primarily needed for insurance purposes.

I followed up with Disney by emailing the results of the appraisal and copied to Majesty Jewelers. I confirmed that everything was in order. The alexandrite gemstone was real and Majesty Jewelers was indeed a reputable merchant. It was a "win-win" outcome all around. Two years later, I had the loose gemstone made into the custom man's ring I had always wanted, designed by my favourite goldsmith, Mr. Jost. It was re-appraised by IGL Laboratories and the replacement value was increased to a more appropriate $28,000 Cdn, reflective of the market value and scarcity of the alexandrite gemstone.

The depletion of this new source of investment quality alexandrite from Brazil turned out to happen quicker than expected. The following year in 2014, my wife and I had another family Caribbean cruise with her siblings, again going back to St. Maarten. This time, my wife's sister, Bing, wanted to go to Majesty Jewellers to see whether she could find some alexandrite jewellery that she could afford. Alexandrite was also her birthstone. She managed to buy a lovely pendant with a very nice 0.42 carat alexandrite gemstone at a very reasonable price. But the store no longer had any jewellery with alexandrite greater than 0.5 carats. All the big gemstones, one carat or more, were simply no longer available. Quality alexandrite will continue to be scarce and expensive.

AN EXCELLENT OUTCOME

Collecting things can be a very enjoyable endeavour and if you happen to be so fortunate to collect the right things at the right time, then it can also be financially rewarding. This means collecting things that you like and that may hopefully become rare and desirable; ie. collectibles that are valuable today and will appreciate over time. This won't happen if you chose to collect beanie babies or golf balls with logos of all the courses you have played. It might happen if you had collected the right vintage comics like the first issues of Spiderman and Star Wars. There is a lot of crappy stuff not worth collecting. But people are strange and they will continue to collect all sorts of things they like, whether they have value or not. They collect things simply for their own enjoyment. This applies to us too. We collect beautiful gemstones for the sheer enjoyment of owning them, and not to show them off. Well, maybe to family and friends. It has been a very good way to spend our time and effort!

Like the alexandrite gemstone, imagine the transition I went through from that cheap guy who paid only $600 for an engagement ring for his future wife to this fool-hardy guy who didn't even think twice in spending $21,000 US for a single small gemstone for himself, not knowing for sure if it was real or fake! Good thing, it all turned out well. This journey in gemstone collecting has been a wonderful experience, but it may not be over yet! If I can only find a stunning Burmese ruby that I can afford! I think I will have to become a millionaire first! Dream on!

Chapter 7

POTPOURRI

<u>Story #27</u>

GROUP OF SEVEN NUDES!

I once took a course in watercolour painting at the University of Calgary where they had nude model painting sessions. I think that was what attracted me to this course. It was something I had never done before. Now, I could never draw a woman (or one that looked any good), let alone a naked one! So, this was very interesting to me not because I liked looking at naked women, but because it was art! Painting the human anatomy requires precise skill and technique. It was supposed to be one of the most difficult and challenging things to do in watercolour painting to get the skin tone and brush strokes right the first time. Unlike oil paintings, you could not simply paint over your mistakes!

Now before you get any wrong ideas, this was strictly on an artistic and professional level. No, I was not there to ogle the models, although some were very pleasing to the eyes. I could see my wife rolling her eyeballs when I said this. Men are often so pre-occupied with the naked female form. The class was made up of six men and 12 women of all ages, abilities and backgrounds. Everyone worked very hard on the shapes and proportions, light and shadows, and in getting the skin tones, textures and colours right.

I wouldn't say that my initial sketches in class were any good. They certainly didn't flatter the models. But I was really motivated to learn more. So, I got books on human anatomy from the library and I practised. The first nude I painted was a small one composed from a Calvin Klein ad for perfume. The woman was holding a towel in front of her and she had her head arched way back seductively. I took artistic liberty in painting her without the towel, using my vivid imagination. When the painting was completed, I asked my wife what she thought of my first attempt. She knew that I had been working on something, but she didn't know exactly what I was doing. She had this strange look on her face, a look of disapproval, as if she was thinking, "what had her crazy husband painted?"

"Well, what do you think?" I asked. Personally, I thought that it wasn't too bad for a first attempt.

"It looks kind of pornographic." She said, looking at it critically.

"What do you mean it's pornographic? It's art!" I exclaimed.

"Well," she continued, "This woman has no clothes on!"

I told her that it would be very difficult to do a nude study if I had put clothes on all the nudes I drew! She was not impressed. Well, back to the drawing board. The next nude composition came from a lingerie ad. By now, my wife was convinced that I was indeed obsessed with nudes. But then again, weren't all men? The second painting was a much better effort. The woman I painted even looked like a woman, although she looked much older than intended! The best part of her body was how well I painted the fingers on her hand. Were you thinking of something else? I even got a "not bad" comment from my wife which from her was high praise! I showed this work at my next class and they thought it was a good effort. One of my male classmates even went so far as to ask whether the woman in the painting was my wife! No, I said sadly. I asked and she would only say "in your dreams!" Well, a man could always dream.

Today, I still can't paint a decent looking nude. I tried my best, but it was still not good enough! Someday, when I become a better artist, I hope to do a series of watercolour painting entitled "The Group of Seven …. Nudes". It's a catchy title, isn't it? Right now, my paintings are not good enough to be shown. To date, there have been no masterpieces painted. Strangely, people still ask me, even to this day, when am I ever going to get these nude paintings done. It looks like I may have to try again after I finish writing this book!

Story #28

WHAT INHIBITIONS?

We were born naked and we will die taking nothing with us. What is it that makes some people very inhibited with nudity and others not concerned whatsoever? What's the big deal? Should this be a thing that should really matter in life? The answer depends on what you were taught and exposed to when you were young. Some cultures and religions have very strict views and restrictions on nudity. I lost my inhibitions as a teenager when I was in high school over 50 years ago. What happened then would be considered socially unacceptable today, but the social views on public nudity were very different decades ago.

I went to the High School of Montreal located on University St. just opposite McGill University. This school closed in 1979 and it was converted to an Adult Education Center teaching English as a second language. When it was a high school, the building was designed like an "H" with the boys segregated on one side and the girls on the other. The library was located in the middle of the H, shared by both sides. Unique to this school, it was one of a few in Montreal that had a swimming pool where students were taught how to swim in addition to other gym activities. There was a very strange rule when the boys went to their swimming classes. All the boys were expected to be completely naked. Only our gym teacher, Mr. Shetler, wore swim trunks. We were not allowed to wear swimming trunks. Nothing, just bared ass naked! This didn't apply to the girls taking swimming classes as they were allowed to wear swimsuits to maintain their sense of modesty and decorum. Not so for the boys as we ran around like adolescent naked jaybirds! The rationale for this total exposure was that the swimming lessons would be quicker as the boys could dress and undress very quickly without having to worry about wet swimming trunks. White towels were already provided by the school.

A lot of male genitalia was exposed, in all shapes and sizes, circumcised or natural, hairy and otherwise! And when the water in the pool was very cold, you could see everyone's pecker shrivel up to the size of a child's wee. The first lesson was awkward with all this nudity, but when we got used to it, everyone thought nothing more about it. Boys would be boys and we would have loads of fun when we were drying off, snapping our wet towels at all those naked butts! Just as people who chose to go to nude beaches were comfortable in their own nudity, we lost our inhibitions about showing off our naked bodies in public. All the boys who went to this High School of Montreal will remember their naked swimming experiences. Could this even be possible today? Never! With all the news of child molesters and sexual perverts and inappropriate touching, a whole class of naked young boys would just be too much of an open invitation for sexual misconduct.

Having lost my inhibitions at a young age, I was comfortable being nude. It was no big deal. A body is a body and everyone is born with one. I even had those dreams that I was walking naked in public just carrying a shopping bag. Everyone else was fully dressed and looking at me. Was I seeking attention or was I a closet exhibitionist? Sigmund Freud once said that, *"Dreams are disguised fulfillments of repressed wishes."* Maybe I was dreaming of a life being a nudist? Nudity should not be a mystery. Maybe that was why I seemed to be infatuated by nudity. But then again, weren't most men?

Story #29

ADVENTURES ON NUDE BEACHES

My wife and I always had diametrically opposite views on nudity. Pat went to a Catholic high school and she was taught by nuns. You could guess how conservative and proper her nature would have been. Nudity was a very private matter for her, and it was never to be gratuitously exposed in public. This made for a very interesting life together. When you don't have any inhibitions, what is there for you to do? I could have walked around naked in the house, but my wife would say, "Stop being so obscene and put some clothes on!" Obviously, my nudity didn't have the desired effect I had hoped for. In our society, it was also against the law to display any nudity in public areas. The exception to this were the nude beaches where clothing was optional. I had never been to a nude beach and I always wondered what it would be like to be surrounded by so much nudity. After all, life events were to be experienced, trying different things whenever the opportunities presented themselves.

My first experience with nude beaches was at Wreck Beach in British Columbia. located just adjacent to the campus grounds of the University of BC. Our family had just moved to Edmonton and we visited Vancouver the following year. One of the sights was the beautiful landscaping and gardens around the university campus. I had heard about this clothing optional beach that was frequented by the students at the university. I said to my wife, "Wreck Beach is close by. I'd like to see what this beach is all about." She had heard about this beach too, and she replied, "You go ahead. I'm going to the gardens." Our two sons, ages 7 and 9 years old, decided to come with me, maybe liking a beach over a garden. Then off we went. The trail down the ravine to the beach was narrow and steep, and we enjoyed the challenge of hiking down the winding trail. As it was a sunny summer day, we were dressed simply in tee-shirts, shorts and running shoes. When we reached the beach, I saw large tree logs strewn haphazardly all over the place. There were many people, mostly young and fully naked, sunbathing amidst the logs. We had arrived! The people walking about were in varying stages of being either partially dressed or fully undressed. Those in the water were totally naked, frolicking in the surf.

I decided that we should walk along the waterline, getting our feet wet. Since we didn't bring any swimsuits and we looked quite conspicuous with our clothes on, I told my boys to strip naked to join the crowd. The boys didn't seem to mind, as we rolled up our clothes in a bundle and carried our shoes. We blended in instantly. I had never seen so many naked bodies in all sizes, genders, shapes and colours. Nudity certainly had its own unique allure. I have always said that you couldn't say you had officially been to a nude beach unless you were also naked there with the masses! I could cross this off my bucket list! I didn't know what memories my sons might have remembered, when their father made them walk naked in public. But at least, they could say that they had officially been to a nude beach, and experienced first-hand all that nudity. After a nice "eye-opening" walk along the beach, we dressed and returned to the university campus where Pat was waiting for us at the pre-determined place. "How was the beach?" she asked. "Great! You should have been there." I responded. "Lots of naked people all over the beach!" My wife just shook her head. She would recall this incident afterwards as the time I had tried to corrupt the moral values of our sons!

The second time occurred many years later when our sons were away at university. Pat and I decided on a trip to Hawaii, starting off in Honolulu. While there, we did the regular tourist stuff - shopping, sight-seeing and walking on Waikiki beach. When we visited the Big Island, we decided to try something different by visiting all the black sand beaches we could find. Because of the ongoing volcanic action on this island, there were supposed to be many beaches with black sand before they bleached in time to become the lighter grey and beige sand beaches. Imagine a beach with totally black sand!

These beaches turned out to be very hard locations to find. Other than the Punalu'u Black Sand State Beach which was prominently listed on the map and where all the tourists went to see, the other beaches were fairly obscure and not readily accessible by car. One beach which was shown prominently on postcards no longer existed as the lava flows still prevalent on the Big Island had wiped it out the previous year. I asked around and I managed to get a few "prospects" from the locals and we were off in our rented car in search of these black sand beaches. We visited dozens of beaches, but most of them were just regular sand and not the jet-black fine sand we wanted to find. We did find a couple of beaches which had gray sand and there even was a green sand beach. Volcanic black sand beaches change in colour from jet black to different shades of grey and even to white given enough time, like thousands of years.

We were down to our last possibility and the location looked really out of the way. We were driving some remote back dirt roads that were cut through the dense forest, thinking that we were lost. There was absolutely nobody around. When all of a sudden, we broke through the shadows of the forest and into a clearing and onto a paved road, and I exclaimed,

"Where did all these parked cars come from?" We found the beach. Apparently, we had come from the back roads which people rarely used. We parked our car and we started down the path from the embankment to the shoreline. As we got closer to the beach, I could hear the ocean surf and I could see that the sand was jet-black, blacker than any of the other beaches we had seen to date. The ocean was pure blue with immense three to four feet surf waves pounding the beaches. I could see people sunbathing and splashing in the surf. This was great, finding this elusive beach!

I was admiring the scenery when I heard my wife exclaim. "Oohh! Naked people!" I walked down a little further where she was and sure enough, I joined her in saying "Yes! Naked people!" By this time, we couldn't help noticing the white naked bodies glistening starkly against the contrast of the pure black sand! The images of white bodies on black sand were really surreal, and I said this, of course, from my purely artistic perspective. We had stumbled onto a nude beach and one of the few in the world with jet black sand. I was kind of worried what reaction I would get from Pat because she wouldn't have come here if she had known it was a nude beach. I sensed that she was uncomfortable with all these naked people around and I was a bit uncomfortable because I was still dressed in my loud Hawaiian shirt and shorts. I looked every bit like a tourist and an overstuffed chicken! I had inherited these very skinny chicken legs from my father and I thought that they would be less conspicuous if I were naked!

Did we look out of place? Yes, certainly if we remained dressed. Did my wife strip this time and joined the crowd in their naked freedom? I wished, but sadly no. To make a long story short, we didn't stay long. We turned around and we went back to the car. So officially, my wife has never been to a nude beach, even though she saw one. What a disappointment! However, if you ever plan to visit the Big Island, here's the secret I will share with you about this unique black sand nude beach that is frequented mostly by the locals – it is Kehena Beach located on the southeast tip of the island! It was almost obliterated one year when a lava flow from the active volcano on this island swept across the beach. It still exists today as a nude beach! Hopefully, you will find this unique black sand nude beach and indulge in a life of naked and carefree freedom.

Story #30

AMETHYST HUNTING IN SEOUL

This story is about gemstones and buying amethyst in Seoul. My wife and I have been collecting gemstones and making custom jewellery for quite a while now. It is something we like to do together. The last time I was in Seoul on a work assignment, I had taken a tour with some of my team members and their wives to see the major sites of Seoul and surroundings. Typical of these Korean tours, you would end up in government sponsored stores selling either ginseng or amethyst. We ended up at a place selling amethyst, the purple gemstone for which South Korea is famous for having. I didn't mind going there as I was always open to learning something new about gemstones. Because I knew very little about amethyst, I usually asked the most senior person there, who spoke English, what made for good quality amethyst? It turns out that colour was the main determinant factor and that the Asians liked a deeper and darker purple, while the Americans liked the lighter purples. I managed to find a very nicely coloured and relatively large trillium cut amethyst gemstone weighing a hefty 9 carats. I liked it because the stone was very sparkly and gemstones of this size are rarely cut in the triangular trillium shape. I was surprised that I could get this stone for a mere $200 US! In other words, amethysts are cheap compared with the other types of gemstones my wife and I had collected. I bought it immediately. Then I proudly showed it to my colleagues and their wives who all said it was a pretty stone, but maybe thinking that I was a real cheap guy for spending only $200 for the wife and then boasting about it! As it turns out, no gemstones I ever got for my wife ended up to be cheap as she has very expensive and specific tastes when it comes to jewellery. Of course, she wanted to have this stone set as a pendant in 18 kt white gold which ended up costing another $1,900 for a custom design from our goldsmith! So, the math didn't quite work out as expected. But it is a stunning piece of jewelry nonetheless and it looks expensive even though I know the stone is cheap. I kept reminding myself, "Happy wife, happy life"! I think my wife is happy, but I never know for sure.

On my last trip to Seoul, my good friend and work colleague, Wayne, came this time with his wife, Patricia, who had never been to Seoul. Now Wayne was feeling guilty that he never bought his wife any expensive jewellery of any kind in all the years they have been married. And I did my best to make him feel more guilty by reminding him that Patricia is a beautiful woman who deserves the best. Besides, he had loads of money so why was he being so borderline cheap! Both of them had heard about the big amethyst which I had bought for my wife and what a great deal I got. They wanted me to take them to this place to see if they could find something special Patricia might like. We ended up going there over the week-end. When we walked into the store, the salespeople looked at us somewhat surprised as no one else was there at the time. They wondered where we came from since it wasn't from their normal busloads of tourists. I told the saleslady who spoke English that I was there the last time from a tour and that I had bought some amethyst from them. Now my friend and his wife were here looking for amethyst jewellery as well. That got their full attention immediately and they knew that we were there to shop unlike the other tourists who may have been brought there against their will! They started to show Patricia all their amethyst jewellery and loose gemstones in their showcases.

I was sitting by myself at another counter while Wayne and Patricia were checking out the goods in the showcases. A short, elderly woman, no more than 5 ft. tall, came around the counter, smiled at me in greeting. Koreans were so polite. I smiled back. She pulled out a box and placed it in front of me. Then she proceeded to take out several bundles of rolled tissue paper. The saleslady who spoke English came by and she mentioned that this woman was the owner of the store and that she wanted to show me her "private" collection of loose amethyst gemstones. The owner didn't speak English, but she must have found out from her staff that we were there to buy, so she was going to show me her best stuff. The saleslady also cautioned me that these special gemstones from the owner's private collection were also very expensive. Whereas the amethyst jewellery on display in their counters typically went for $20-30 US per carat and for which we could get a 30% discount from their retail price. The top-end amethyst gemstones being shown to me were for "special" customers as they cost $200 US per carat and carried only a 20% discount. I just shrugged and gestured to her to show me what they had. I was definitely interested as I had never seen what high end, very expensive amethyst gemstones would look like.

As the owner unrolled the tissue paper, I could see many large and beautifully proportioned amethysts that were uniformly in a deep purple colour. I selected two very large gems which were particularly eye catching and I called Patricia over to take a look. She hadn't found anything of interest yet. She wanted something special for a pendant. One of the gemstones was a traditional oval cut with the facets cut on the underside and it was the darker of the two gems. The other was an India cut which had additional facets cut on the top of the gemstone which made it very sparkly. Patricia liked the first gemstone because of its deeper purple colour, but I told her that everything looks great under these high intensity lights above the counter. I took the gemstone she liked and walked away from the lights into the shadows and asked her what she saw. "Nothing. Just a darken gem. No sparkles at all." she said. I told her that the clarity and cut of this gemstone must not be as good as we think since it could not capture enough light through the gemstone to be reflected back to her. Something like trying to capture light looking through a dirty window. I then tried the same thing with the India cut gemstone and it clearly sparkled even in the shadows. Patricia could clearly see that it was the better gemstone.

The owner, the saleslady and Wayne were watching us as we did this and it became obvious that Patricia wanted to buy this gemstone. But wait, she was not finished. Patricia also wanted matching gemstones to be made into earrings to go with her pendant! I thought this might be a problem, but the owner dug further into her magic box and came up with two smaller oval shaped gemstones which matched the intense purple colour and the sparkle of the big gem perfectly. Everyone agreed that this was indeed a rare and wonderful set of matched gemstones and that it was meant to be for Patricia to own them! Now it was the time to get into the price negotiations for these gemstones. They weighed the gemstones and they totalled 30.5 carats with the big gemstone at 18.5

carats! That is one humongous gemstone! The retail price at $200 US per carat would make it $6,100 US, less 20%. They offered to sell these gemstones at $4,900 US. Now Wayne happens to speak impeccable Chinese, while my Chinese is just barely passable, but I managed to say to him that I think we could get these gemstones for $4,000.

The saleslady was listening and she asked coyly, "Why are you fine gentlemen not speaking English?"

Koreans can be both polite and discrete. We just smiled at her. Wayne replied to me that he wanted to offer $3,800 and I indicated sure, why not. Wayne told me later that he initially wanted to offer $3,500, but he thought that this might be too low.

When the owner heard about the counter-offer, she was like any typical Asian woman, "Aiya, how can you offer me such a low price! I cannot make a living at this price! I cannot do it!"

Then she gestured, made a few faces of exasperation and stomped away waving her arms as if indignant. Now all this was in Korean, so I guess that was what she said. Meanwhile, the saleslady pleaded with Wayne to do better on his offer, first to $4,000, then to $3,900, but I have to give credit to Wayne. He was tough and unmoved. He repeated, "No. That is my price."

In hindsight, the owner didn't really have much choice but to accept. There are not many customers who would appreciate and be willing to pay for the best quality amethysts. And she definitely could not let a $3,800 sale walk out the door. So, the price we negotiated was an excellent deal at 37.7% off the asking price. At the end, everyone seemed to be happy, including the owner. Even though she didn't speak a word of English, she paid me the ultimate compliment. She pointed to me, then to her eye and gave me the universal thumbs up! After all, I did pick out her best amethyst gems. What a great time and experience shopping with good friends and learning something new at the same time. Life is full of such memorable encounters. But now, I can't call my good friend cheap anymore! Better still, neither can his wife!

When they got back home, Wayne had to do what I did and spent a few thousand more to have these gemstones made into a stunning pendant necklace with matching earrings. All in all, this was a very small price for a very happy wife!

Story #31

PEKING DUCK

In 1998 when our boys were attending universities in other cities, Pat and I finally took a trip to Hong Kong where my wife grew up. Pat wanted to attend a re-union with her old high school friends from many years ago. Surprisingly, they all still remembered each other and they had a great time when they got together. Hong Kong was famous for food, especially its fresh seafoods. While I was there, I wanted to eat a fresh fish steamed with ginger and shallots. Fishermen will tell you that when you cook a freshly caught fish, the flesh is so sweet and tasty. There were many restaurants that had large aquarium tanks that displayed all types of fish swimming about and you could choose one to eat. We went to this one restaurant that was high end judging by its décor and the white tablecloths and uniformed wait staff. After being seated, the waiter invited me to see the fish. The place had a huge 20-foot long tank covering one complete wall. I watched with particular interest as this one pink-red fish was aggressively chasing all the other fish in the tank. This was the fish I wanted to eat as it was healthy and strong, full of vigor. I pointed at the fish, at least a two pounder, and said "That's the one!" The waiter nodded in appreciation that I may have selected the best fish in the tank.

Two men with nets on 10 feet poles had to coordinate their efforts to corral and capture this fish as it was fast and elusive. When they finally caught it, the fish was brought over to me in a plastic tray. It was still flopping around at my table. This was the very tasty orange-roughy species. The fish had been weighed and the waiter quoted me the price to have this fish prepared steamed the way I wanted. "$1500 Hong Kong dollars" he said in a matter-of-fact way. "What?" I thought, doing a quick mental conversion to Canadian dollars. $300 dollars for a fish?! Apparently, this particular fish had become quite scarce, being overfished because of its popular reddish color. The waiter seeing my surprised expression on my face understood immediately my hand gesture waving it away. I was blunt even in my sign language, as if I were saying, "Throw it back in the tank!" Poor fish! I was still obligated to choose another fish which the waiter helped me choose a more common and cheaper grey one. It still cost me $70 Cdn to eat! I didn't know fresh fish could be that expensive! At that price, it was nevertheless very tasty, but that was the last time we ever ate fresh fish again in Hong Kong.

After this "fishy" culinary experience, we travelled to China. Even though I was born in China, I left when I was a toddler. This was the first time I went back there and Pat's friends had booked a couple of tours into

China for us. The tours were quite inexpensive, like $3300 Cdn for two people for two separate trips into China – a total of 15 days including airfare, tour guide, bus, food and accommodations. My only difficulty was that these tours catered to people from Hong Kong, and they were conducted entirely in Cantonese.

Now my Cantonese is only one-quarter fluent at best, and when you are stuck on a bus full of people who know you can't quite speak the language, they don't talk to you, and vice-versa. Having gone from my work position where I was always in control of the language and in charge of the situation, I had absolutely no control of anything. I had to be totally dependent on my wife to translate. To be truthful, I didn't like this at all! I certainly had a lot of time to practise my listening skills. I distinctly remember sitting in the back of the bus, trying very hard to understand what the tour guide was saying. Pat was interpreting where she could, but everything was spoken so quickly. Listening was hard work. Finally, I got so tired of listening and tuned out the whole conversation as a lot was lost in the translation. I declared to myself that, "There was too much Chinese being spoken in China!" It was logical, eh?

These tours generally patronized the government sponsored hotels, pharmacies, outlet stores and restaurants. While we were in Beijing (formerly known as Peking), we were scheduled to stop at this restaurant at the Fei Xia Hotel, which supposedly had the best Peking duck not only in China, but in the entire world! This was one of the highlights of the tour since the Peking duck dish originated in China. This restaurant was so proud of its reputation for this dish that they gave everyone a bronze medallion after the meal to commemorate the event. The Peking duck in Calgary was not bad, so we were looking forward to eating the "real" thing, and the best in the world at that. When the duck arrived at our table, everyone in the group dug in. What a disappointment! The skin was not crispy, the duck was fatty and the meat was quite chewy and tough. It occurred to me that we in North America have been spoiled in the quality of our meats. Our chickens and ducks were grain fed and they were very tender to eat. The chickens and ducks in China, however, were tough and sinewy from all that running around, being free range birds! Anyway, this particular duck was really difficult to chew.

We all sat there quietly trying to digest this duck and complaining about its toughness. It was the worst that anyone of us had eaten in our lives! This much of the Chinese I understood, as complaints in any language sound like complaints! When the meal was finished, the restaurant passed around these comment cards to get some feedback from each table. This card was passed from each member of our table until it came to me. As I was the designated "foreigner" in the group, coming from Canada, I said "why not", since no one else wanted to make any comments despite their dissatisfaction. My first reaction was to write "This duck really sucks!", as it certainly was a terrible duck. But on second thought, I decided to temper my comments and wrote down in English something to the effect that "Having come all the way from Canada, I found the Peking duck to be a disappointment. But that everything else was okay". When the note was passed back to the waitress, she took it immediately to the person I assumed to be the manager of the restaurant. Several others joined him while they were looking at my handwritten comments written in English instead of the normal comments they would get in Chinese.

Then it dawned on me. I was still in Communist China and this was a government sponsored restaurant. That was why the rest of the people at our table, who were from Hong Kong, were smart enough not to openly criticize the government in anything, even something as innocuous as a chewy duck. Quite unlike the foolhardy Canadian at their table! I even signed my name on the comment card which was another dumb thing I did! A brief thought flashed by that I might not be able to leave China. I could see the newspaper headlines - "Duck dissident detained in China indefinitely!"

I was really glad then that I hadn't gone with my first instincts, otherwise I still might be in China today! Good thing it was a different era back then when China was just opening up their country for tourism and they were more tolerant and accepting of foreigners. The tour director kept reminding us to be mindful and respectful of what we did or said, but he never warned us about the pitfalls in eating Peking duck! My travels to different countries seeking unusual culinary experiences have certainly been interesting to say the least.

Story #32

DO YOU BELIEVE IN FATE?

This is the story of how my younger son, Tim, became a doctor. Being a doctor wasn't his first choice of profession as his primary interest was in computer science ever since he was a youth. He was very good in mathematics and in computer programming and much of what he did was self-taught. He had always wanted to create a computer game, so he learned Turbo Pascal, the dominant programming language at that time. Tim was consistently a straight A student, but in his third year at McGill University pursuing a Bachelor of Science degree with an Honors in Bio-Chemistry and a Minor in Computer Science, his marks dropped to B^+ average. My wife and I were puzzled and we asked, "What happened to your marks?" He told us that he had spent too much time developing his computer game based on the popular TV show Sailor Moon, a female Japanese anime character. He did all the artwork and animation with well-defined heroines and monsters and plot lines. He found ways to download the sounds and dialogue directly from the Sailor Moon cartoons shown on TV and he programmed them into the game. It took him a lot of time and effort to complete two levels of action. Recognize that this was done over 25 years ago when computer animation was in its infancy.

There was no 3D animation nor the detailed graphics and seamless action that current computer games display. He showed me this version of his game and it was very impressive. His animated artwork was head-and-shoulders better than the simplistic graphics and animation of the Donkey Kong or Pac Man games of that time. He had put his game on the internet and asked for it to be beta tested by people interested in trying it out. This got him many "volunteers", especially young girls who liked the female Sailor Moon character. Tim had included a counter on his program to see how many people were actually playing his game. When the counter recorded more than two million users, he thought this must be wrong. There couldn't be that many people wanting to play his game, even if it was for free.

Well, it turned out to be true. He got a notice from his internet provider that there was too much traffic on his account and that they had to charge him much more for the service. His game was seemingly that popular for both guys and girls! It was going to cost too much, so he decided to shut it down. If he was more business-wise astute, he should have contacted the Sailor Moon company and demonstrated his unfinished program that already seemed to have universal appeal. There wasn't a computer game like this on the market and Tim could have ended up on an alternate career path being a computer game developer and programmer. But Tim did this only because it was something he wanted to do, and not to make money from it. Besides, he still wanted to finish university to get his degree. Some might consider this to be a lost opportunity. But in life, windows of opportunity opened and closed all the time. You just had to recognize and seize upon these events whenever they occurred. Tim was like me in this respect. I would like to try something different to see if I could do it and whether I was any good at it. Like writing this book, when it is completed, I might stop writing altogether with just the satisfaction knowing that I could do it! Money was always secondary. Strange, but true.

Going back to the story, Tim would often visit his grandparents when he was attending McGill in Montreal. His grandfather knew that Tim was planning to become a doctor. He would say, "Tim, why do you want to be a doctor? They work so hard and they have no time for families." He had based his comments from his experience with his own doctor who regularly worked 60 to 70 hours every week, including week-ends. This comment must have influenced Tim as he still had the choice either to go to medical school to become a doctor or to pursue a master degree in computer science to become a computer programmer. When it was time for him to submit applications to get into various medical schools, instead of sending multiple applications to five or six universities across Canada like what most other candidates did, Tim sent just one application to the University of Alberta. Fortunately, his application was good enough for him to be granted an interview.

Tim had done all the necessary preparatory work to get into medical school. His university marks were top-notch. His MCAT score was excellent and he had spent the time doing the pre-requisite volunteer works and public service at various organizations. But so did everyone else aspiring to become a doctor. There were over 1000 applicants vying for the 100 open spots at the University of Alberta and every applicant had exemplary and comparable qualifications. What would differentiate Tim over his other competitors? Tim had envisaged that the combination of his computer skills with his medical knowledge could result in the development of superior diagnostic tools using technology to identify the possible diseases people might have. He was ahead of his time as medicine and science did not mesh too well back then, and being strong in mathematics and computer programming were not traits doctors needed to be successful. I coached him not to stress too much on his computer technology competency even though he was good at it. Then Fate came into play during this all-important personal interview process.

Normally, there were two senior doctors assessing his qualifications with a third younger physician attending to gain experience. On that day, one of the senior doctors was absent, so there was really only one senior doctor for him to impress. Since all the candidates had similar academic qualifications, the questions were more focused on individual interests and personal achievements outside of academic studies. A simple question was asked by the doctor, "What books have you read?" Now, this was a trick question as Tim did not read any books other than computer manuals. However, he did read one book which my older sister had given me to read years ago and which I had passed over to Tim to read. It was entitled: "Surely You're Joking Mr. Feynman!" This book was about the Nobel prize winning nuclear physicist, Richard Feynman, who was a very colorful person marching to his own drum.

Tim replied, "I read a book." And he stated the title. Indeed, Tim was speaking the truth. He had read **a** book! The senior doctor's eyes sparkled as he said, "Great book, wasn't it?" "Yes, it was," Tim replied, smiling back. Bingo! Alignment of thoughts and interests. It was Fate and Tim was lucky to be accepted into the only medical school he applied to. It was meant to be. Who could have imagined that a single obscure book with a quirky title would be the difference maker that resulted in Tim becoming the first doctor in our family!

Story #33

A SOULMATE FOR OUR SON

My wife said that I should stop embarrassing my sons by writing about them. But I can't help myself. This story is too good to be left untold. When my younger son reached adulthood, I gave him some fatherly advice. I said, "Tim, be careful. Some women can be very calculating, and if they want to catch you, they may use sex to trap you!" And I added, "Just like your Mom!". At which point, my wife happened to walk in, overheard our conversation and promptly snapped back at me. "I'm not that kind of girl!" I looked at her somewhat puzzled as I didn't know what kind of woman my wife was thinking I thought she was. After all, I have always been kind of clueless when it comes to understanding women! But I ask all you men out there. Women do have inordinate power over men and sex appeal is the one thing men cannot resist. Is this true or not?! Nature made it this way.

As parents raising children, we want to give them a stable and supporting environment for them to grow and develop. They also need a good education to have every chance for success. When they achieve their own careers and leave home, we don't want them to come back to the nest! We want our children to find someone they will be happy with, get married and have kids. Enjoy life. The children's lives should be better than their parents. Sounds simple enough, but it seemed like it took forever for our younger son to find that special someone, to fall in love and to get married!

I think that it was partially my fault. I didn't give too much advice to my sons, but the advice I gave, they listened to. In hindsight, maybe they shouldn't have taken my advice so literally. For example, I told them that the only expectation I had with any girl that they chose to pursue, was that she had to be smart. They needn't be Asian although I think that's where my wife made her own expectations known. This had something to do with my unproven theory that smart children came from smart mothers. I am a perfect example of this. I don't consider myself super smart, just very tenacious and stubborn. But my two sons are smarter than me because my wife is smart! When my oldest son, Ted, married Alex who is quite an intelligent woman, he was simply following my advice. When Tim was studying to become a doctor, I gave him some additional advice about women. I told him that when he became a doctor, he didn't have to worry about finding a woman as they would come swarming around him like hungry birds. There would be so many that he would have to shoo them off with a stick! Or something inappropriate like that. After all, most parents would love to see their daughters marry a doctor! Right? My wife couldn't understand why someone like me, who had a hard time taking advice from anyone, would insist on giving advice about women, something I professed to know nothing about!

Tim was very inquisitive as a child. For a long period, he started every sentence with "I wonder ... this" and "I wonder ...that." So much so that my wife called him "my wonder boy!" He also had a very analytical and scientific mind that made him cautious and meticulous in everything he did. By nature, he always looked before he leapt and he was hesitant in trying anything new until he got it right the first time! He was a perfectionist and there was no room for him for any trial and error. My wife remembered the time he first saw the Mary Poppins movie. He asked his mother to teach him to say the magical word "Supercalifragilisticexpialidocious", but he refused to learn it syllable by syllable. He made his mother say the whole word over and over again until it was driving her crazy. Then suddenly, the whole word came out of his mouth perfectly at his first try. He was beaming with joy! That was his character. Girls and dating were something new to him. He took my advice about women literally and he stayed at home, spending most of his time on his computer, waiting for all these girls to seek him out. This was not a problem when he was in his twenties and still in university. As parents, we networked with our friends and relatives to seek out prospective girls for him to meet. That didn't go too well. After a few times, we were told to stop and to leave him to his own devices to find someone. But when he became over thirty years old, after having built up his career and purchased his first house, I started to become very concerned. I even had a dream about it! In my dream, I met this nice Asian girl with long, flowing black hair, and typical in my dreams, all the women are beautiful! In talking to her, I found out that she was 27 years old and unattached. I asked what her name was. It didn't register with me, so I had her spell it out, which she did. I recalled thinking that this young lady might be a very nice match for my son, ... just before waking up.

When I woke up, I remembered her name! This was very unusual as most people don't remember their dreams, let alone an exact name. As I described this dream to my wife, she asked. "What's her name?" I replied without any hesitation, "Ling-Wa Lo." Now don't ask me where this name came from. It was also a good thing that I was dreaming about someone for my son and not a woman for myself. If I did dream about another woman, why would I even tell my wife? I might not be the brightest lightbulb out there, but I was certainly not the dimmest either! I couldn't be that dumb. My wife just smiled and said, "Don't worry, dear. He will find someone eventually." Coincidentally, I knew a colleague, whose surname was Lo. He just happened to have a daughter. I was afraid to ask him whether his daughter was named Ling-Wa. Now that would have been too coincidental and weird when dreams become reality!

This matter must have really stuck in my subconscious mind. It got to a point where Pat and I were driving downtown and we were stopped at a traffic light. This nice-looking Asian girl walked across the street in front of us. I said to my wife, "Wouldn't she be a nice girl for our son?" Pat just looked at me, rolled her eyes, and said, "You are so pathetic!" I guess I was, looking at strangers on the street as possible mates for our son!

I finally told my son that even though his ideal woman is out there waiting for the opportunity to meet him, how can she find him if he kept hiding inside his home? To his credit, he tried dating in earnest. First, he joined this dating service called "It's Just Lunch", specifically targeted for professional people wanting to get together. After a few dates, it became apparent that the number of eligible Asian women in Calgary who were compatible with him was fairly low, and the dates became just exercises in having lunches at expensive restaurants. Then he tried this "Six Minutes Dates" club where you sit down with a girl and ask each other many personal questions to see if there are any "sparks". The bell rings after six minutes, and then you go to another table and start this process again with another stranger. Nothing happened there as the girls tended to be younger, not as educated as he was, and they were really more interested in just having a fun time dating. My son mentioned that the girls were somewhat intimidated when they found out he was a doctor. They would say, "What are you doing here? You're a doctor!" So much for my advice!

I was beginning to wonder whether my son was getting too picky as he got older and more set in his ways. Maybe he was expecting too much perfection from his future partner? So, I asked him what he was looking for in a woman. Well, this list I called "Tim's super specifications", was quite long. First, this woman had to be attractive. This makes sense as there should be some common attraction to draw couples together in the first place. Then she had to have a university degree to meet his smartness criteria. Good, he was still listening to me. She had to have a sense of humour. So far, so good as there are many girls who have these qualities. She had to be Asian. My wife was happy to hear this, but this started to narrow the field. Then she needed to be somewhat "sporty", enjoy swimming, biking, playing tennis and other outdoors activities. This was getting more difficult because most of the Asian girls I knew were not that sporty. The prospective field narrows even further. The next item was a real doozie. Because he loved computer programming and games, his prospective mate should preferably have a degree in computer science! Get real! Most people with computer science degrees in North America are computer geek guys. Very few girls take computer science! I almost stopped listening at this point, but he wasn't finished. This woman had to be "low maintenance". I asked him what that meant. He said that she needed to be fairly independent and not the clingy type relying on him to do everything. Finally, she mustn't be prone to saying dumb things! This probably came from all the young girls he met at the Six Minutes Dating Club. Well, with specifications like these, no wonder he couldn't find anyone! No one could be that perfect! That was where Fate played a part in the form of a matchmaker being in the right place at the right time.

Fate took me to lunch one day at the food court downtown, where I bumped into Fraser, a Caucasian engineering colleague whom I hadn't seen for well over a year. We used to work together in the Mechanical department. I was bemoaning the fact that my son still wasn't lucky in love and it was getting harder to find someone as he got older. I was beginning to lose faith in my belief that there was a unique soulmate for each and every person in the world. As it turned out, Fraser's son, who was well in his thirties, recently married an Asian woman, and he thought that one of her bridesmaids would be ideal for my son. At that time, she happened to work in the procurement department at the same company as us. Since Fraser knew her, he was willing to ask her whether she was currently dating or not, and whether she would be interested in meeting a doctor. Cool I thought, "Let's do it!" It should be pointed out that when two engineers decided to do something, we became very single-minded and action oriented. The next day, Fraser got a positive answer. It was then my turn for action. In the meantime, you can say that I had secretly checked up on her – what department she worked in, what she looked like, what she did and whether she was any good at it! After all, this woman might possibly marry my son! As usual, I was getting ahead of myself. I wasn't sneaky, just curious, as any parent might be. I called her and asked her to come to my office to meet me right away. I didn't know if she felt a bit intimidated by me or not, but by nature she was a very brave and independent person. Let me tell you that this first meeting was quite awkward. Even with all my communications skills, how do I discuss something I had not done before? I wanted the conversation to be open and congenial and I definitely wanted to leave a good impression. But in reality, I was conducting an interview. As much as I wanted to, I couldn't ask direct questions like, "You want to date my son? Tell me, what are your qualifications and why are you interested?" Somehow, I managed to communicate with her without embarrassing either of us. Then it was up to my son to take the next steps. It turned out better than expected.

Surprisingly, she met every one of my son's extensive specifications, and more. She adopted Jane as her English name. Her Chinese name, Hui Jie Zi, as far as I am concerned, was close enough to Ling Wa Lo! In the time she dated Tim, she learned to ski and play golf. She played badminton and tennis, roller-bladed, took up ball room dancing, and she knew how to swim, ride a bike and she liked hiking. That more than met the sporty requirements. In my interview, I mean discussion, with her, I found out that she knew of me from the training course I gave at work. She had scored 100% on the course test which was quite impressive for a non-engineering person. This certainly met my smartness criteria. Also, she had a Masters degree in Computer Science!! When I heard that, I was convinced that this was <u>the</u> woman my son had waited for! Young women who had left China by themselves to study overseas and work and develop their careers in other countries had to be very independent and self-sufficient. She definitely was low maintenance. My daughter-in-law, Alex, gave Tim a very valuable sisterly advice. She reminded him that "low maintenance did not mean no maintenance!". And lastly, regarding women saying dumb things, my son had not yet learned that women never said or did dumb things. And if they did, women would never admit it! Only men did dumb things. As my wife has told me many times!

While it took some time and effort, my son finally found his perfect soulmate and equal partner. My wife and I couldn't have been happier and we felt so relieved. Maybe more so for myself! This story is a reminder that no matter how bad the situation may seem in finding true love, there is a person especially destined for you. You just need to keep a positive outlook and have a bit of luck. Life will always be full of unexpected surprises and opportunities.

Story #34

MOVIES WORTH REMEMBERING

This story is about grandchildren. There is immense joy and wonder in the grandparents' relationships with their grandchildren. For those of you who are already blessed with grandchildren, you will know exactly what I am talking about. To be a positive influence on your grandchildren, especially in their formative first five or six years, you have to see them often and be part of their lives as they are growing up. We had this opportunity with our two grandsons whom we saw regularly while they were growing up in Calgary. We would take them out to see a movie every time there was a new animated film or a PG rated movie that was suitable for kids. This was a treat for them as they would look forward to getting popcorn, treats and drinks each time they went. I believed that these treats became more important than the movies.

Movies were excellent ways to teach a lesson or to learn something new visually. We would watch the movies with them, explaining the story and the various characters. – unlike some parents who would use videos and TV cartoons as quasi-babysitters to keep their kids occupied because they were busy doing other things. When there weren't any new movies being shown, we would watch some of the older classic movies on video. Mary Poppins was a great movie for kids with its catchy combination of memorable songs, fantasy, quirky characters, dancing and animation. They learned how to say the magic word "Supercalifragilisticexpialidocious," both forward and backwards! They liked this movie so much they kept watching it over and over again! They saw their first scary Wicked Witch of the West in the Wizard of Oz. That was one really scary looking witch for young kids! They learned what a bully was like in seeing all the bad and intimidating things Biff, the bully, did in all the Back to the Future movies. They even saw the movie, I Robot, where I tried unsuccessfully to explain Isaac Asimov's three laws of robotics to Evan. But I think I was going a bit too far because he was still too young to understand!

We saw the movie Pixels which showed the popular video games that their father used to play when he was a boy. Evan, always the observant and sensitive one, noted that one of the young boys in the movie said some bad things to his grandmother when she asked him to do something else after playing video games. He immediately said out loud in the theatre, "I would never say those mean things to my Nai Nai!" The boys constantly talked about monsters and zombies, so I showed them all the Disney movie villains - like the evil witches and stepmothers from Snow White and the Seven Dwarfs, Cinderella, Sleeping

Beauty and 101 Dalmatians. The internet was a wonderful source of all sorts of monsters and demons. They graduated to real monsters like Medusa and Godzilla and those vicious dinosaur raptors in Jurassic Park. Good thing I could find these monsters on YouTube, and I would preview these monsters with them. Evan would be sitting on my lap on one side and Nathan on the other while we watched these videos on my laptop. I would explain to them what these monsters were all about and which ones were not real, so they would not be scared when we saw the actual movie.

Keep in mind that Evan was six years old and Nathan was only four. They were still very impressionable and a bit too young for the hard-core scary movies like Pan's Labyrinth and the other slasher blood-and-gore movies that were equally inappropriate. My son was rightfully concerned that his boys would get nightmares watching these movies. When we did watch video movies that had monsters, my grandsons would sit on either side of me on the couch. They would have their favorite stuffed animal to "protect" them and a blanket to cover up and hide under during the scary parts. Of course, there was home-made popcorn and juice. So far, so good, as no nightmares had been reported by the boys after watching a number of these supposedly "scary" movies. This worked fine until we saw Coraline, an animated movie which I hadn't seen before. This was my fault in not pre-viewing it. Because it was animated, I thought how scary could it be? All the other animated movies we saw were fairly benign. Well, this movie turned out to be very psychologically scary and it was creepy even for me!

The movie was a story about a little girl who got stuck in an alternate world where her alternate mother had black buttons for eyes. She wanted Coraline to stay there permanently and the only way this could happen was by sewing buttons into Coraline real eyes! Coraline was trying desperately to escape from her evil alternate mother, but she seemed trapped! Evan could understand the story and he really got scared halfway through it and he didn't want to watch it any more. He was very afraid Coraline was going to get buttons sewn into her eyes. Nathan, being younger, was clueless on what was really happening. He just liked the weird Mr. Bubinsky character who was a strange looking old man that held an umbrella while he danced on the roof in the moonlight. I got scared too, just as when I was young, I was traumatized by movies with weird dolls with buggy eyes in them. I could never watch any movies like Chucky the Clown or Rosemary's Baby.

As the boys were having a sleepover that night, we agreed to stop watching the movie in the dark and finish watching it the next day in the morning when it was brighter and less scary. I wanted to show Evan that all these movies usually had a happy ending and that Coraline would find a way to escape her evil alternate mother and not have buttons sewn into her eyes. That was the exactly how the movie ended when Coraline found a way to trick her evil mother and finally get back safely to the comfort of her own home and to her real mother. Since that day, Evan never wanted to see this Coraline movie ever again! He would remember this movie in the same way my sons remembered the first time when they saw the snake-haired Medusa in the movie, Clash of the Titans and she had scared the wits out of them!

When my wife saw how scared Evan was, she was very angry with me and she yelled at me, "You traumatized your sons with Medusa when they were young. And now you traumatized your grandsons. What's the matter with you! You stupid grandfather!" I could only think of the time my father let me watch my first Frankenstein movie when I was young. It had scared me half to death, so much that I was afraid to go to the bathroom when the lights were turned off. I replied with the only plausible thought that came to my mind, "Family tradition?"

Story #35

FORAYS INTO THE WORLD OF AUCTIONS

Someone once said that you went to auctions "to look at other people's old junk!" If the junk was not worth organizing or cataloguing, it would be called a garage or yard sale. If the "junk" was really high end and valuable like an original Picasso, then it definitely would be auctioned off at the prestigious Sotheby's or Christie's. Auctions can be a very exciting experience especially when you are directly involved and bidding on something. You can feel your heart pounding, your nerves on end, your mind racing with anticipation as the auctioneer works the crowd with his rapid staccato. And when you win the object of your desire, you think, "What the heck am I going to do with this?!!"

People went to auctions to look for bargains on things they thought they wanted. Items sold at auctions typically were usually sold at between 20-40% of the auctioneer's estimated value. If you were lucky, the price could be as low as 10% when nobody else was bidding against you, or exceeding 100% if there was a bidding war when more than one person wanted the same item. That's why it is called an auction. Competing bids were solicited and expected as part of its normal process. My wife and I enjoyed going to auctions because we never knew what items would come up for auction and how little they would be sold for. The fun had always been in the search of unexpected finds. Anything and everything could be auctioned – from contemporary to antique furniture, to Persian rugs, to jewellery and paintings, artwork and collectibles, and even to cars and boats. We've seen ridiculous items like a framed print of "Dogs Playing Poker" sold for $15 and a garish oil painting of Elvis on velvet that sold for $50. We've also seen original oil paintings from the Group of Seven painters, A.Y. Jackson and A.J. Casson, go for $12,000 and up. Think of it this way. Throughout our lives, we collect stuff and when our worldly possessions are passed on to our heirs, what do you think happens? Right! They will keep the good stuff and sell whatever else of value they can at auctions! Anything left unsold can be liquidated at garage sales or given away to charities like Goodwill.

There used to be two reputable auction houses in Calgary. Now, there is only one left. At the auctions, they only guarantee that the item as described will be as stated. There is no guarantee that the price you paid was fair nor will they prevent you from being stupid enough to overpay. Items are sold "as is". In other words, "buyers beware" is the rule at auction houses. You must see and inspect the item you are interested in and never purchase anything sight unseen or based on just a photo or description. A diamond ring listed in their catalog will be a diamond and not zircon. An original painting offered will not be a print. Pricing can be as low as $10 for something nobody else wants or it can be a very valuable and expensive item like a natural Columbian emerald pendant appraised at $46,000, but sold at $4,900! Bargains can be had if you happen to be lucky in bidding on something that you actually wanted, and nobody else was in competition with you. It also helped when the item had no set reserve or minimum price on it. We don't go to those transient auctions conducted by outside companies travelling to various cities and renting space at hotels to sell their goods. You can never be sure that there aren't any "fake bidders" planted in the audience bidding just to drive the price up. We learned that the hard way at the beginning before we became more experienced recognizing such situations at different auction venues.

The rules of the auction are very simple. You register to get a bid card and you can bid on anything that interests you. If you win, you pay for the item plus the auction house commission (typically 10 to 25%) and take it home as is. That is why it's very important to preview the various lots before the auction to determine the condition and how much you think it is worth and the total amount you are willing to pay for it. During the auction, contrary to other beliefs, you can scratch your nose, touch your ears and even roll your eyes during the bidding stages. Just don't look at the auctioneer when doing it! We've heard the auctioneer say, "Sir, is that a bid or is your nose just itchy?" To bid, you get the auctioneer's attention by raising your hand or flashing your bid card. This will indicate your interest, that you are in the running. The auctioneer establishes eye contact with you and he will always seek this eye contact as long as you stay in the bidding. At this point, your gestures can be as subtle as a slight nod of your head indicating yes or no. However, remember the cardinal rule – set your maximum limit and stop. It takes discipline not to be carried away with the bidding and end up paying more than you had intended.

If you go to enough auctions, you will get quite good at assessing the value of different items in various categories. We think we can tell real antique furniture from imitations, which Persian rugs are really valued like the silk Tabriz, and we got really good at estate jewellery. We got books on antiques and gemstones and jewellery to learn about them. We watched the Antiques Roadshow on PBS TV to learn what real collectible antiques were supposed to be. Two things became readily apparent at auctions: "There is no accounting for peoples' tastes" and "People will buy junk if the price is right, meaning really cheap!" We have seen lots of ugly stuff being sold. We were often surprised at the amounts of money people would pay for items we would consider junk that we wouldn't take even if those items were given to us for free! But we have been carried away on items that were priced so low, making them too good to be true. I remember saying to Pat one time at an auction, "The price is so low, I don't care if the gemstone is real or not! What a bargain!" What was I thinking of?! Good thing that item turned out to be real. The auctioneer can be very entertaining in his efforts to sell stuff that even he considers junk, "Madam, I realize that this lovely hall table has one leg shorter than the others, but it will be fine if you lean it against the wall!"

I enjoyed talking to people at the auctions. They came from all walks of life. Once, we were sitting next to a man and his wife. They seemed to be bidding on all sorts of things while we were focused mostly on the jewellery on auction. This guy and I would comment as each item was auctioned off, "Not a bad price", or "Nope, paid too much!" as if we were experts or something. Then a matching pair of marble plant stands came up on the block. These were made of real marble, not the imitation marble, and they were very rare and in mint condition. My wife's interest perked up immediately.

"Forget it Dear," I said, "We still have that wooden plant stand from the last auction that I still haven't got around to re-finishing!"

These marble stands were expected to go for about $300-$400 each as their retail price would have been closer to $1000 each if they were sold at a store. The guy next to me bought them at $175 each which was a great price. He didn't even bother to consult with his wife who was sitting just beside him! He just went and did it. "Hey, man, good buy!" I said, knowing that he definitely hadn't planned to buy these plant stands, "Now what are you going to do with them?" Auctions have always been unpredictable and you never know what bargains you might find. Remember, "Other people's junk could be your treasures!" I should know because I have a lot of these "treasures".

Story #36

HOPELESSLY IN LOVE

During my courtship with Pat, I wrote the first poem. I was much younger then and crazy in love. The second poem was written the year I married her. These were the only poems I ever wrote! I was such a romantic! Perhaps, you would like to share these thoughts with the love-of-your-life?

To the One I Love (1970)

Of all the people in the world,
You are the special one.
Because it's you and only you that …. I love.
I ask myself why I love you.
In truth, I cannot honestly say.
All I know is that …. I am
And loving you is both
Pain and ecstasy.
When I am far away from you,
Your spirit haunts my mind
Until the urge to see you becomes
Unbearable.
Then when you are with me once again,
I become insatiable.
To gaze upon your beauty, to touch your
Soft skin, to look into the mysteries

Of your eyes
Only drive me on and on until
The desire for you is sheer agony –
I AM HOPELESS!
Hopelessly lost .... and
In love with you.

There Is No One in the World I Love More *(1971)*

My Love,
You mean so much to me.
Without you, my life would be
An empty void.
I would feel lost like a person
Existing without a purpose –
A living corpse whose dreary
Shadow creeps across a world
Stripped of joy and happiness.

But you are here and
My heart feels your tender love.
As the darkness surrenders
To the light,
I see clearly that
You are mine
And I am yours
And together, we shall always
BE ONE

Chapter 8

ENGINEERING STORIES

Story #37

"ELEPHANT IN THE GRASS!"

In my previous position as the Chief of the Mechanical Department of a major engineering company, I would interview and hire many engineers with varying mechanical equipment experience to fill the positions needed. I was also looking for a particular individual to eventually replace me. I had intended to move up the corporate ladder and to become the manager of engineering in charge of all the engineering disciplines – process/systems, civil/structural, piping/layout, mechanical, electrical and instrumentation. I couldn't do this until I found a suitable replacement for myself. This person, of course, had to have a very high level of mechanical engineering skills, and be well versed in all sorts of mechanical equipment and piping systems. He, or she, needed the people skills to manage the staff of 30 people I already had in my department. Most importantly for me, my replacement had to have a sense of humor as work should never be overly serious all the time.

There was an excellent candidate who was working for the parent company in the USA. Shashi was a mechanical engineer who had graduated in India and he was interested in relocating to Calgary. In my initial discussions, he seemed to be as people-oriented as I was in our management styles. His technical qualifications were solid and he seemed perfect as my future replacement for my position as the mechanical department manager. But I was not sure if he had a sense of humor that came from not taking things in life too seriously. During the interviews conducted over the phone, I asked the typical questions normally expected, like why he thought that he was the best person for the job, his main strengths and weaknesses and the accomplishments he was proud of. He was answering them with ease and without any hesitation. So, I threw him a curve as I wanted to know the depth of his sense of humor, or whether he even had one!

"Tell me a joke and it has to be a clean one!" I asked. This request was simple enough. There was a noticeable pause and hesitation. Maybe he didn't know any jokes that were not dirty or inappropriate. Maybe he was thinking, "Why is he asking me such a dumb question?" He certainly didn't expect such a question. Sensing his discomfort, I continued. "I want to see if you have a sense of humor. Let me tell you a joke that I liked." I proceeded to tell my joke about the elephant in the grass.

Question:
"How did the bull elephant find the female elephant in the tall grass?"

Answer:
"Very nice!"

It was simple, sweet and definitely clean despite its sexual nuance! There was still silence, so I asked him to email me his joke when he could think of one. He did later on, but the joke couldn't have been too good as I didn't remember it! I gave him credit for at least trying. I realized that there weren't too many people who shared my strange, and somewhat weird, sense of humor!

Shashi was hired to be my second-in-command and he was mentored by me for about one-and-a-half years before becoming the Mechanical Department Chief. During this time, a new metallurgy and welding group was created from nothing and it became the pre-eminent source for this specialized expertise that was second-to-none in all of North America. This group grew to 12 specialist engineers that surpassed the metallurgy and welding department of the parent company which had provided this expertise in the USA and for projects world-wide. When I was promoted to Manager of Engineering, the company was in a period of intense expansion, growing from 600 to 2500 people in a couple of years. During that time, the Mechanical Department grew from 30 to 120 people under Shashi's capable stewardship. When you think of 120 mechanical engineers just in a single department, most people wouldn't even know so many engineers, let alone all of them being in the same mechanical discipline. It was unheard of in any other major engineering companies in North America. At the time, no one thought that this was anything special. But in hindsight, it was indeed a remarkable achievement that would never happen again!

Story #38

ON BEING LUCKY

B eing lucky is often a random event. Sometimes, you are lucky without even knowing it because you had always taken your good luck for granted. Take the example of the schools I attended. When I went to the High School of Montreal, it was the closest school in the district where I was living. Little did my parents know that it was the best high school in all of Montreal at that time. All the rich Jewish families sent their kids there to get the best education possible. Half the students in my class were Jewish. As a result, I got a great education! When it was time to go to university, the historic McGill University was conveniently located just across the street from my high school.

I never fully appreciated how fine a university it was then and what a great reputation it had, and still has, for its engineering program. When people found out that I had graduated from McGill, they were usually impressed. McGill, in Canada, was similar to the reputable ivy league Harvard or MIT universities in the USA. I usually tell people that I was simply lucky to be living close by. There were never any thoughts of going to any other university. I was going to McGill, period! I could have lived in the adjacent district where I would have had to go to Baron Byng High School and then ended up going to Sir George Williams University (now Concordia). There was nothing wrong with these schools other than few people know of them. There is a cachet in having graduated from one of the best universities in Canada. It gave me the solid engineering education which made me successful in my career as an engineer.

At a McGill alumni luncheon in Calgary in 2007, I found out that McGill was ranked by MacLean's Magazine to be the No.1 university in all of Canada for the last three years in a row. The following year, its ranking moved up to be the 12th best university in the world and the No.1 university in all of North America, beating out a lot of the fine universities in the United States! Yet in a locally conducted survey of all the universities in the province of Quebec, McGill was only ranked sixth! Go figure! I guess this survey had included all the French speaking universities in the province and they were all ranked higher than McGill! Without really knowing how lucky I was way back then, I know now and appreciate how fortunate I had been.

<u>Story #39</u>

DUMB THINGS ENGINEERS DO!

One time at work during a team building session as the lead engineer, I tried an unusual technique to get people to open up to each other by sharing some of their very personal experiences. I said that in our lifetime, we all have done something really dumb. I asked them to think about such an incident and whether they would be willing to share that experience with the rest of the team. To break the ice, I told them the dumbest and most dangerous thing I ever did. As far as I knew, I was the only person brave (my wife would change the word "brave" to "stupid") enough to have disconnected a 220V stove live! Think about it: fooling around trying to disconnect the high voltage wiring to the stove while the 220V power was still on. Stupid might not have been a strong enough word! I could have been electrocuted! Then this story would never have been written.

My wife and I were living in a rented flat after we got married and I had to disconnect the stove that very day because the new appliance was being shipped ahead of time. I needed to move the old one out of the way. I couldn't find the fuse panel to turn off the power and I couldn't ask the landlady as she was away that day. But being a qualified mechanical engineer and having some basic knowledge of electrical wiring and circuitry, I decided that I could disconnect the stove while the power was still on. In hindsight, that was really, really dumb! A little knowledge can be very dangerous! Being much younger then, I felt invincible as I thought I knew what precautions I had to take. After all, I was a trained engineer! Stoves back then didn't have these nice 220V plugs which you could just safely stick into or pull out of an electrical socket in the wall. The power cord simply consisted of three sheathed wires – black (power), white (neutral) and green (ground) – with their ends stripped bare to allow them to be connected or disconnected directly onto the appropriate power terminals at the back of the stove. Touching the exposed ends of any of these wires during this process would have been extremely dangerous.

Before proceeding further, let me explain how inherently dangerous electricity can be. For those of you who have had the unpleasant misfortune of being shocked by 110V, that was just a minor shock that wouldn't necessarily kill you. It is nothing compared with being zapped by 220V, or worse, being struck by lightning. Electricity will always seek its shortest path to ground. When you see lightning strike a tree, the electricity is simply going through the tree to the ground. Yet the power and force of the electrical shock can split the tree apart! People who have been fortunate enough to survive and not die from a lightning strike can tell you how painful and damaging an experience it was. I have never been hit by lightning so I don't really know how bad it could be, but I have been shocked by 220V. I remember this incident very vividly. I was probing with a screwdriver trying to adjust something inside a blue-printing machine at work. Yes, another dumb thing I did! I inadvertently touched the power contacts, not realizing that this machine was actually powered by 220V and not the common 110V. The force of the shock hurled the screwdriver across the room, embedding it like an arrow into the wall. The resulting electrical arc coursed through my body, cutting my forearm in the process (yes, high voltage electricity can cut and sear flesh) and it caused my heart to beat like crazy. It really hurt! It took over an hour for my body to calm down. I didn't know how reckless and foolhardy I was when I tried to disconnect the stove before I was zapped with 220V.

In my mind, I could disconnect the stove safely. All I needed to do was to prevent myself from being grounded when I touched the wires. The human body is a very good conductor of electricity, but if I could be insulated somehow, then the electric current had nowhere to go and I couldn't be shocked. That was the extent of my safety plan! Dumb! Instead of the heavy-duty rubber gloves the high voltage power repair guys used to protect themselves, I only had the kitchen dishwashing variety rubber gloves. My knee pads were made of foam rubber and my running shoes had rubber soles. I even placed a rubber mat on the floor, anything to help keep me from being grounded. The pliers and the screwdriver had insulated handles. Remembering how people who were struck by lightning had electrical burns from any metals they happened to be wearing, I removed my ring, watch and belt. I felt protected. Yes, double dumb! I slowly unscrewed each wire from the stove, then very, carefully using the pliers only on the sheathed part of the wire and never touching the bare metal end, I pulled the first wire out of its socket making sure it touched nothing as that would have been disastrous. The exposed end of the wire was then very cautiously wrapped with electrical tape to provide some "insulation" that would prevent it from touching the bare ends of the other wires as they were pulled out and likewise wrapped.

First the green ground wire and then the white neutral wire came out. I recalled a bead of sweat trickling down my forehead as I touched the black wire. I left this as the last wire to be disconnected as this was the "hot" one and the most dangerous. I then realized what a crazy thing I was doing, but I didn't have the sense to stop! I don't remember how, but I managed to disconnect all the three wires and taped them up. But I was not out of danger yet. I then had to squeeze the three taped wires closer together (but still not touching) so the power cord could be pulled out of the 1" diameter grommet hole in the back of the stove, taking care not to scrape the tape covering these wires and accidentally touch any metal part of the hole cut-out. This last step seemed to take forever and I was feeling totally stressed. Once out, I had to carefully spread out the wires again and tuck it safely against the wall in the corner out of the way. It was done. The stove was disconnected and it could be removed. I was extremely lucky not to have been electrocuted. I should have been. I remembered something my father had told me, *"When it is time for you to go, then it is time for you to go."* Thank goodness it was not yet my time! Luck had been on my side. Ironically, the following day, I found the electrical fuse box panel in an obscure place located inside the linen closet. Who was the dumb person who put it there! It must have been done by some guy! The team members who heard this story were amazed that anyone, especially an engineer who should have known better, would have done such a dumb and dangerous thing.

Surprisingly, there was another person (yes, another engineer), close to my age, who wanted to tell the group about his "dumb" thing. He talked about how he had found a smarter way of putting up his annual outdoor Christmas tree lights. These were the old-fashioned incandescent bulb lights which had to be checked for burnt out bulbs that always needed a few to be replaced before stringing them up. Normally when he did this outdoors, it was always on a cold day and his fingers would freeze. As engineers were always problem solvers, he had decided this year to check the bulbs indoors in the warmth and comfort of his home. What a great idea! He brought all his string of lights into his living room and laid them on the floor. After plugging them in, he could tell immediately which bulbs needed to be replaced. This was progressing well, and he was thinking how smart he was when he smelled something burning. Apparently, these outdoor lights were hot (which is why they were only meant to be used outdoors) and they were melting the synthetic fibers in the carpet.

It was a classic case of Murphy's Law: *"When several things can go wrong, the one that would cause the most damage will be the one that will go wrong."* Well, the lightbulbs he was changing were bright red in color and his living room carpet was a nice light beige. When he unplugged the lights and lifted them off the floor, his lovely carpet was all permanently dotted with red marks all over the place! His wife was livid! What a dumb engineer! To calm her down, he had to replace the entire carpet at a cost of several thousand dollars. Now that was a very dumb and costly mistake. It sure beat mine for dumbness, but I definitely took the top prize for stupidity!

It is strange that I have never encountered a woman who would openly admit she did anything dumb. Is this a peculiar male trait to do dumb things and then be proud of them? Guys have no qualms in saying, "Look at me. I'm really dumb!", like it was a badge of honor and our exclusive right to do dumb things! All of us must have done something super-dumb in our lives. Care to share your moment of dumbness? Be brave and tell someone like your partner or even your friends. The worst thing that can happen to you is being laughed at! And no one has ever died from embarrassment!

Story #40

ANYONE CAN DO ENGINEERING!

It's true. When I was a mechanical engineer in my early years before I became a project manager, I learned how to design, specify and evaluate all sorts of mechanical equipment. Unless you were designing something that had never been done before, most engineering designs have been well documented and covered by established codes, standards and design methods. You just had to know what they were and how to apply them correctly. If you could find an experienced person who could show you precisely how certain things were to be done, you would learn very quickly and avoid all the time and hassle learning from your mistakes. Most engineering tasks are quite straight forward and easy to do once you know what is needed to be done. It is not like brain surgery requiring a very level of skill and knowledge that only a brain surgeon can do, although some engineering tasks can be very complex and challenging.

To demonstrate this point, I once showed a non-engineering person, Jack, how to do a pump evaluation. He was working in the procurement group helping me purchase some centrifugal pumps which I had specified for a project we were working together on. The bids from multiple pump manufacturers had come in and I was going to evaluate their submissions and recommend the best pump based on performance and price. As part of the pump vendor submissions, performance curves were requested to show how efficient each pump would be at various flows and discharge pressures. The pump operating with the highest efficiency at the desired flow and pressure would require the optimal size of motor, making the unit very cost effective to operate.

Pumps from different manufacturers are like people in that there are never two exactly alike. They all had their strengths and weaknesses. As there were many pump suppliers world-wide, 12 bids were received. Now, Jack had an inquisitive mind and he asked me how long it would take for me to do the technical evaluations to decide which pump was the best. Noticing his interest, I said, "Not long. Do you want to learn how to evaluate a pump?" Jack perked up immediately. "Sure!" I showed him how to read the performance curves after plotting out the desired operating point for each pump offered. These performance curves would show what the pump's discharge pressure and capacity would be at various diameters of the pump impellers could be cut to. The impeller was that spinning part of the pump that generated the flow and discharge pressure. The proposed pump was deemed to be too large if the impeller was cut to its smallest diameter, or it was not large enough if the pump impeller was at its maximum size. The efficiency at this operating point will be shown and the size of the electric motor required for this pump had to be calculated. I showed him the simple formula to calculate the required horsepower to confirm the motor size needed. If the pump operated inefficiently, the motor and the associated operating cost would be greater than a pump with a better efficiency. Those inefficient and costly units would be eliminated right away from further consideration. This typically removed at least half the proposed pump offerings.

"Then you can make a selection based on pump efficiency and price?" Jack asked, thinking that this was way too simple just looking at the pump curves. "Almost," I replied "Of course, you have to make sure that everything else has been included according to the data sheets and specifications so that the pricing from each manufacturer can be comparable." Then I said, "The next step is to check the pump at run-out conditions." Jack looked puzzled. "Run-out conditions? The pump can run away?" I told him that the pump impeller would be cut to the diameter that would match the required flow and discharge pressure. However, this operating condition could change and run-out conditions occurred when the pump was operating at its maximum flow and its minimum pressure for its selected impeller diameter. This usually occurred when a flow control valve failed to modulate and it failed in the fully open position. The pump had to be sized to operate for its full range of its capacity for that impeller size and not trip out the motor. This was done by taking an arbitrary run-out point on the performance curve and noting its operating efficiency. Then the required horsepower was re-calculated at this run-out condition. If the resulting motor was the same size as the one calculated for the normal operating condition, then this pump selection was good and price and performance would dictate, everything else being equal. If not, a larger motor would be required and this would increase the cost of the motor and the associated operating cost for that pump.

"That's it?" Jack asked. I could see that he was already making the selection which I would have made myself. "Darn right!" I replied. "Nothing to it!" This engineering task was nowhere close to brain surgery, as the steps were defined and the methodology set. I never knew whether Jack used any of this new-found knowledge in checking the pump selections made by other mechanical engineers. But now, he knew what to do for a technical pump evaluation. Life is like this. Someone shows you how to do something. You learn to do it and it becomes part of you!

I believe that there is a reason why you meet or have met certain people in your life and how they contributed to making you the person you are today. In Montreal after graduation, I had been working in a small consulting engineering firm for a number of years. As one of only four engineers working there, I learned to do everything from designing piping systems, specifying and purchasing equipment, writing specifications and contracts doing field supervisions and start-ups and managing multiple projects at the same time. It was a great experience that gave me this "can do" confidence that I could do anything. It certainly didn't hurt that my mechanical engineering education at McGill University gave me all the basics and skills in various elements of design. But most importantly, it taught me how to solve problems, any problem, by using a structured and analytical approach based on logic and accepted principles. There was nothing I felt I couldn't do given enough time to learn and the right information. Except for maybe brain surgery!

When I moved from Montreal to Edmonton, I joined Associated Kellogg Ltd (AKL) which was the Canadian office of the much larger engineering company MW Kellogg based in the USA. This company was so large that its engineering department had to be segregated by specific discipline, each responsible for the designs associated with that type of engineering work. For example, piping systems were done by piping mechanical engineers, structural works were done by structural engineers, electrical designs and equipment by electrical engineers, and so forth. I was hired as a mechanical engineer responsible for designing and specifying all the different types of equipment required on the projects. Most of the equipment was for major refineries and petrochemical plants and they were much larger in size and more complex than anything I had purchased in my previous small consultant engineering office working on pulp and paper and boiler installation projects.

I was hired as the mechanical lead for a major project required by Imperial Oil of Canada, the Canadian office of the global Exxon Corporation. My first job was to specify a massive centrifugal compressor that needed to be driven by an 8000 HP asynchronous or induction electrical motor. If these words sounded foreign to you, they were also foreign to me as I had never specified such a large and complex rotating equipment. I had no expertise in this area, but I knew where to get it. Normally, in the mechanical discipline, there would be experienced engineers specializing separately in rotating equipment, fired heaters, pressure vessels and heat exchangers and packaged equipment.

Because the electric motor was part of the overall compressor package, I had to go to the electrical group to get them to do the motor data sheet and the accompanying specifications. That was the first time I met Sharana who was my counterpart as the electrical lead for the same project. He didn't know me from a hole-in-the-wall as we had never met nor worked together. I showed him the requirements Imperial wanted for the motor and I asked him when he, or anyone else in his group, could do the electric motor data sheet and specification I needed to complete the mechanical package for the compressor. "I'm busy now, but I'll get to doing this when I have more time," he said somewhat dismissively to me. Since I had a deadline to get this major piece of equipment out for bid, I said "That's okay. Let me do the motor data sheet and I'll send it to you for review." Sharana just looked at me somewhat incredulously and nodded, but maybe thinking "Get real! A mechanical guy doing electrical work on a complex electric motor that required a lot of control safeguards? Good luck!"

Here was the secret to my success. As an engineer, I always considered my technical skills to be just so-so. I could do all the design calculations and follow the ASME codes in designing pressure vessels and size other mechanical equipment following set procedures, but I was never the smartest nor fastest engineer out there. I was just okay. There were always other engineers who were technically superior with much more knowledge and experience. But I had two very good skills. For some reason, I knew who these "go to" people were who had the answers and I knew how to get the right solutions from them. Secondly, because my father was always people-oriented, I was likewise the same. I respected the skills of these highly specialized individuals and I trusted the information and advice they gave me. They would always help me because they knew that I would do the same for them whenever they needed.

I had already established a good relationship with the mechanical department chief at MW Kellogg and he was a very experienced and knowledgeable in his position. When he heard about the compressor I needed to specify, he told me that on another project they had just purchased a compressor almost identical in size to the one I was doing and it also had an induction motor. He sent me the detailed purchasing specifications that day. My final secret, I was a great copier! These were the technical specifications for both the compressor and motor which I would not have known how to do as they were done by compressor and electrical experts at MW Kellogg.

Included were the data sheets and specifications for that complex 8000 HP induction motor with all the necessary "bells and whistle" safety options listed. I copied the details of this motor on our data sheets and sent it off to Sharana the next day.

Well, this got his immediate attention. He was really surprised at getting the motor data sheets so quickly that he dropped everything else he was doing and started to review the technical details in earnest. In his mind, he must have been thinking that this mechanical guy who could do electrical work was too good to be true! In reality, I was just very lucky. He found nothing wrong with the motor data information I specified, or more correctly, I copied. Sharana and I became close working colleagues and good friends afterwards. I dreaded to think what could have happened if I had screwed up. Sharana would have never trusted me as a person nor for any of my technical abilities as an engineer. More importantly, I would have lost a life-long friendship. It was hard to imagine that such small and seemingly innocent events in life could have had these deep and lasting implications!

Story #41

IT'S A MAN-MADE WORLD

B eing in Fabricland, a fabric and sewing accessories store whose main clientele were women, it helped reinforce my observation that it was very true when someone said that "It was a man's world." What this quote really meant was that "It was a man-made world." I had often wondered what were the things that were entirely made by women without any involvement or support from men? Other than giving birth which was essential for the survival of humankind, what else is the sole domain of women? I was surprised that I couldn't come up with another example. Modern science and cloning and gene/DNA manipulations could even one day make women replaceable in artificial birth reproduction. That would indeed be a sad day for humanity when scientific and biological advances replace the human process of pro-creation. Everything you see, use and touch in this world has been wholly or partially been influenced or made by men. If you asked my wife, Pat, she would tell you that she could definitely live without me as men were very dispensable. Look at all the widows in the world! You have heard the joke, *"A man was good for only one thing, and she already took out the garbage!"* Without men, however, the world would not have all the modern comforts, achieved from scientific and medical advances and the extensive infrastructure we have grown accustomed to in our civilized world. On the other hand, we might not have all the pollution, the wars and strife and weapons of mass destruction created by men. This is the reality of our life. While science and technology helped advance our standard of living, they might also be the cause of our future demise.

At Fabricland, I looked at all these different rolls of fabric. They were made by machines designed and built by men. The many colorful designs and patterns were also made by men. The sewing machines, reams of cloth, needles, scissors, buttons and thread were made by men. Even the cutting tables and cash registers were made by men. Everywhere you looked and every physical thing you saw and touched had a man involved in its existence. Sure, women used the materials made by men to make their own clothing and their fashion designs could be equally or better than what men could do. But they couldn't have done any of this if men hadn't provided the base materials and machines. I qualify this statement to include female engineers and scientists. I could see that the world would be a very different place without all these man-made products everyone took for granted.

We indeed live in a man-made world. The innovation and productivity of engineers in producing countless material goods and facilities have been mind-boggling. Engineers are like the worker bees in a bee colony, hardworking and industrious, creating the products and maintaining the infrastructure. Engineers are usually invisible in the background, until some catastrophe occurred. Then they become indispensable as the ones who must solve and correct the problems, whatever they may be. Without engineers, we might as well go back and live in the Stone Age!

To the engineers of the world, be proud of the fact that you are the engines of our society and civilizations. You may be invisible, but the world we know today could not have existed without your invaluable innovation and contributions!

Story #42

STANDING BEHIND YOUR WORK

I have always wondered why very few stories or TV shows have been written about engineers. There were countless shows on the trials and tribulations of doctors, lawyers, law enforcement and emergency responders. The only TV shows that specifically focused on engineering were the ones detailing the marvels that were engineered or the catastrophic disasters that occurred because of negligent or faulty engineering. Stories about doctors, lawyers and law enforcement were more common because people could directly relate to their own personal experiences in getting sick or being injured, or being sued and going to court, or having interactions with the police. Few people had stories involving engineers unless they happened to know someone who was an engineer, or they happened to be one. The life of an engineer seemed boring compared with doctors and lawyers and many other professions. Engineers were seen to be equally as boring as accountants!

The work done by engineers had been absolutely essential in creating and maintain the technological innovations used to build our infrastructure and civilizations, providing the comforts people casually took for granted. The world would be a much different and harsher place without engineers implementing the scientific advances. How many people could say that if they didn't do their job properly, they could die as a consequence? Construction workers and high voltage repairmen could be exposed to daily dangers that could potentially injure or kill them when safety protocols were not followed. A surgeon who made a serious mistake while performing an operation, would not die, but his patient might. The lawyer who did a poor job defending his client in court would not end up being sentenced to death, but his client might be. Accountants could never die from crunching numbers on a balance sheet. Engineers typically wouldn't directly be involved in testing the things they designed and built, but sometimes they had to.

This story shows how dangerous engineering work can be, even to the point of being life threatening. Nova Gas was a major supplier of natural gas which was transmitted across the country via a 24" transmission pipeline. The pressure of this line was very high at 500 psig. (3446 kpag.) and any leaks or ruptures from such a line containing highly volatile and explosive natural gas would be catastrophic. By the time the gas reached the residential homes, the pressure had been reduced to a manageable 100 psig. and then further reduced to be safely used by the furnace and cooking appliances. We have all heard in the news how dangerous it was to have a gas leak in a house which subsequently blew up the whole building as a deadly consequence.

Such critical lines were difficult to shut down as this would be a major disruption in cutting off the supply of natural gas to many areas served by the pipeline. New connections into this main feeder line were generally done by "hot taps" which could be done while the line was active and still in use. These connections would have been much easier and safer to be made if the gas line could be shut down and its contents emptied. Hot taps were specialized procedures traditionally done by pipeline companies who had the expertise and experience in doing such dangerous work. Not all hot taps were dangerous. It depended on what the pipeline was carrying. If it were high pressure steam, even at an equivalent 500 psig., any release of steam due to a leak or rupture could injure personnel, but there would not be any explosion and fire. A hot tap on a 500 psig. natural gas line was one of the riskiest things to do because of its explosive potential.

Without getting too technical, what was exactly done for a hot tap? In this case, a new 6" branch line was needed to be connected to the existing 24" supply line. This required a special pipe fitting called a "weldolet" to be welded directly onto the 24" line. Both the top and the base of the weldolet had beveled edges for welding, and the bottom of the fitting was contoured to sit flush against the circumference of the 24" diameter pipe. Once the bottom edges had been properly welded onto the main header, a flanged connector fitting was welded to the other end of the weldolet. Then a flanged shut-off valve was bolted into place. A specialized hot tapping machine was bolted onto the other end of this valve. This hot tap machine had a metal cutting tool on a shaft that could be extended into the open valve to cut the required 6" circular opening in the main supply line. Everything had to be sealed to prevent leakage of any gas during this operation. Once cut, the pressure in the line would push the 6" disc against the cutting tool as it was retracted back into its machine housing. Then the shut-off valve was closed. Voila! Hot tap done. All this sounded simple enough. What was so dangerous about this? The critical task was the actual welding of the weldolet directly onto the main gas line. The welding procedure and every task associated in doing this weld had to be perfect. There had to be no possibility of creating leaks of any kind during the hot tap.

Author's Note:
Normally, I tried not to be too technical in my description of complex engineering processes and I wanted to use common everyday examples that most of the non-technical readers could relate to and understand. But sometimes, that was not possible in

explaining basic engineering concepts and terminology. My wife read this story about the dangers of hot taps and judging from the questions she asked, I knew I was fighting a losing cause getting her to understand the engineering complexities. Questions like, "What is buttering? Is it like buttering a piece of toast?" or "What is a flange?" and "What does a hot tap machine look like?" and "What does psig mean?" It is a common unit (pounds per square inch gauge) used to measure pressure I assumed most people would know these terms. Stephen Hawking, the famous physicist in writing his book "A Brief History in Time", commented that the inclusion of one mathematical formula would lose half of his readership. The inclusion of more mathematical formulae would lose the rest of his readers! But he couldn't write his book without mentioning $E=mc^2$. Similarly, this story could not have been written without mentioning any engineering terms. Hopefully, the technical content I have included will not have the same effect!

People know that welding is required to fuse two different pieces of metals by "melting" them together using extreme heat at between 6000-8000°C. The most common image is someone in a welding helmet with darkened eye filters shielding the welder from the blinding light and sparks flying off the welding electrode tip. Welding required high energy and heat to create a molten pool of liquid metal in the fusion zone between the metals to be welded and where filler material from the electrode was deposited between the adjoining surfaces. The resultant weld would have the same, or better, properties and strength of the welded steel. The area surrounding this liquid fusion zone is called the heat affected zone (HAZ) which will be "softened" during the extreme heat generated by the welding process. If this heat affected zone became too large, the integrity of the metal pipe could be compromised. For a high-pressure gas line operating at 500 psig., the gas could blow through the softened HAZ, igniting and exploding immediately during the welding process. The key variable for a safe hot tap was to minimize the heat input specified in the welding procedure that reduced the size and depth of the HAZ affecting the pressurized pipe, but still be sufficiently hot enough to end up with a proper and solid weld. One mistake in this welding procedure could be the last one made!

The following summary lists some of the technical considerations and requirements associated with the hot tap procedures. These details are included to show how complex engineering can be and pre-cautions engineers take to ensure that their designs work as intended and are ultimately safe to use. These are included to give those readers who want more technical content. For those non-technical readers who are not interested and who could not care less, skip this listing and go to the following paragraph!

Engineers are trained to be exacting and precise. There cannot be any short-cuts or compromises in the design when the public safety is at risk. Nothing is assumed and every variable is checked and re-checked. Things like:

- Ultra-sonic or X-ray testing to confirm the residual wall thickness of the pipeline in question at the location where the hot tap connection is to be made.
- Mill test reports to confirm the materials of construction and metallurgy for the pipeline and the weldolet.
- The design and operating conditions for the pipeline.
- Piping and thermal stresses at the hot tap location.
- The heat loss calculation by the flowing fluid in the pipeline as this will affect the heat input needed in the welding procedure to achieve a proper weld.
- Finite element analysis (FEA) and thermal pressure calculations.
- Metal Inert Gas (MIG) welding using tempered bead buttering technique.

- Calculation of the required area of the heat affected zone (HAZ)
- Size and type of welding electrodes to be used.
- Calibration of the welding machine being used.
- Qualification and testing of the welder.
- Buttering weld cool down rate followed by dye penetrant examination to test for under-bead microcracking of near quench welds.
- X-ray and hardness testing of the finished welds.
- Hydrotesting or x-ray examination of the welded joints to confirm compliance to code.

The Big B Engineering Company was retained to design and execute this critical hot tap operation. It was rarely ever done by outside engineering consultants or independent welding companies. Fortunately, this engineering company had the services of Mike H. who just happened to be one of the best welding engineers in private business in all of North America. He was mandated to specify the welding procedure and to coordinate and supervise the hot tap using experienced welders from the Big C Welding Company. If anyone outside an established pipeline company could do this work safely, Mike was the man!

The condition of the existing pipeline was checked to confirm its metallurgy. Then it was tested to determine the actual wall thickness at the proposed connection point. The intent was to determine how much reserve pipe wall thickness (or corrosion allowance) was available. Calculations had to be done to determine the minimum wall thickness to be left intact based on the flow conditions of the natural gas in the pipeline. The intent here was to minimize the depth of the molten pool during the welding to prevent too large a softened HAZ that would weaken the integrity of the piping to withstand the pressure. Thermal heat calculations were done to determine the level of the heat input need during the welding process. This was necessary as the flowing natural gas inside the pipeline acted as a heat sink which could draw too much heat away from the welding process resulting in poor quality welds. This was a delicate balancing act to ensure proper welds were made correctly the first time. Faulty welds would have to be ground out and removed and then re-done. This was equally as dangerous as welding and it was something to be avoided on a live natural gas pipeline.

It was decided that the MIG (metal inert gas) welding process was the best using the tempered bead buttering technique with 1/8" diameter welding rods making multiple passes. This would minimize the size and depth of the HAZ especially when the first "buttering" weld passes were made directly onto the pipeline surfaces. Trial tests welds were done in a controlled setting to ensure that the welding machines were properly calibrated as any faulty heat input setting could have serious repercussions. The two welders assigned to do the welding were pre-qualified that they had the experience and "steady hand" to do the welding correctly and consistently.

The big day arrived and everything was in order to do the work. The weather even cooperated, being cloudy with no rain. The actual location was 200 yards outside the main gas processing building. It was chosen to be far enough away that if there were an explosion, the plant would not be destroyed in the process. It was that dangerous. As per the mandated safety protocols, a fire truck had to be brought in in case of fire. It was parked next to a protective concrete abutment next to the main building well away from the potential blast circle. A poor young kid was hired to be the designated "fire watch." This position was totally useless if there was ever an explosion. It must have been his first job. He was given a portable fire extinguisher and his duty was to stand close to the welder to douse out any fires caused by the welder. He didn't realize that he had placed his own life in danger. Mike was at the site to oversee the preparations as he was responsible for the welding procedure and how this hot tap was to be executed. As this work was going to start in the afternoon and run continuously through the evening and suppertime, the team were given a special dinner which was catered in. They were asked what they wanted to eat and they chose filet mignon and lobster! Like condemned men giving their last wishes before the execution! Could this be their last supper? It certainly seemed like it. At least, they were well fed!

Wayne the welder, from the Big C Welding Co., was ready. The young fellow clutching his useless fire extinguisher was standing close by, watching nervously, not knowing exactly what to expect, and hoping nothing bad would happen to him. As Wayne proceeded to make the most dangerous "buttering" weld bead passes on the pipeline, he felt the presence of someone behind him. He stopped and looked behind him, removing his welding mask to see who it was. He was surprised to see Mike, with his welding mask, leaning over his shoulders. Mike was the last person he expected to see as most engineers would have taken cover in a safe place.

"What are you doing here? I thought you would be hiding out with the firetruck where it was safe!" Mike ignored his brusque comment. "I wanted to see the shape and size of your first pass weld." Mike had developed an empirical formula that calculated the HAZ and the depth of penetration of the welding arc by simply looking at the weld bead. The shape and size of the first weld bead Wayne made looked very good, just as Mike had expected to see. Wayne felt reassured that Mike was there to confirm the results immediately. Two sets of eyes were definitely better than one. Each welding pass was tested to ensure that there were no micro-cracks before the next weld bead was overlaid on top of the previous ones. The welding proceeded safely and methodically without incident, everything being executed exactly as planned and specified. The Big C Welding company eventually took this proven hot tap procedure and used it successfully in all their future business doing this specialized and high-risk work!

This demonstrated that when you have the right people with the right qualifications, doing the right things, then only right outcomes would be achieved. The Big B Engineering Company never knew how big a risk they actually took doing this dangerous hot tap. It was something the company had never done before and for a mere $100,000 in fees! If there had been an explosion, the consequential damage would have run into hundreds of millions of dollars that could have bankrupt the company along with the loss of its reputation from the number of lives lost. They were lucky. But most often, you had to be good in the first place to be lucky!

Mike, in his typical wry English humor, said that "It is not every day that I got the chance to stand next to the welder with the potential to blow myself apart." For my part, I always remembered this story as it was the only time I made an engineer "stand by his work", literally and figuratively! Mike, of course, would say that he volunteered willingly, with no second thoughts whatsoever in putting his life on the line! He was that confident!

<u>Story #43</u>

A MILLION DOLLARS BONUS – NOT!

When I was the Manager of Engineering at the Big B Engineering Co., the Canadian operation of the global engineering and construction firm Bechtel based in the USA, I had the rare opportunity to realize a million dollars bonus for doing a simple three months' worth of work. This never came about, as sometimes, things were not meant to be, no matter how much we wanted it to be. This story is about what could have been.

My engineering team across the disciplines was very experienced, seasoned and knowledgeable, and our collective engineering design expertise was second-to-none, capable of competing with all the major engineering firms in the world. Our design specifications and standards were solidly built upon the Bechtel corporate standards which have been the design basis of their many successful projects worldwide. Their documents had been enhanced and updated to reflect the cold weather conditions in North America. The resulting specifications and standards were lean, effective and "fit for purpose". Here is an example to describe what this meant.

When I was designing and specifying the API (American Petroleum Institute) pumps typically used in refineries, I liked the Shell Oil company specification for their pumps because it was a very concise and clear document detailing what was basic features were really needed. It resulted in a good quality pump that met most standard refinery needs. Yet in the course of 10 years, this six-page document became 20 pages long. Each time something went wrong with the pump or new controls or enhancements were needed to improve the operation of the pump for some specialized condition, additional features were added to the basic standard requirements in the specification. It was questionable whether these extra enhancements made the basic pump any better since they would actually apply only to about 5 to 10% of all the pumps that were purchased. This certainly increased the cost for the 90% of the basic pumps most refineries would have been satisfied with. Specifications and standards needed to be reviewed and updated periodically to ensure that their requirements were truly optimal and "fit for purpose" and that additional or extraneous features were removed when not needed, or to be deemed optional instead of being made mandatory across the board for every pump purchased.

We had already updated and revised the Suncor specifications and standards they used as their design basis for their oilsands operation. In particular, we updated their welding procedures to reflect the latest technology, materials and methodology. Statoil, the big French engineering company, was in joint venture with Suncor on one of their projects. They wanted to have their specifications and standards reviewed and revised to meet with North American requirements and procedures. This was a relatively easy task for our company as we already had the talent in every engineering discipline to review their design standards and to make the appropriate adjustments and revisions. This task took the team only three weeks to do and Statoil was very pleased with the results. The best part for them was that we only charged a minimal $80,000 since they were partnering with Suncor, our long-term customer. Normally, we would never give away our collective intellectual property for such a give-away fee. Statoil got a great deal.

Somehow, Imperial Oil Ltd. (IOL) heard about how the Statoil specifications were upgraded to meet the North American standards. One of their project managers approached me to see if we were interested in doing a similar exercise for their corporate company design and operating specifications. This, however, was no small thing. Imperial Oil was the Canadian operation of Exxon Corporation, the largest refinery company in the USA and the set of standards and specifications they wanted us to review and update were the Exxon

Imperial Basic Practices (IBPs). These specifications were the gold standard for designing major oil refineries Exxon used world-wide in the design and operation of all their facilities. Everything that was designed and constructed in accordance with these standards would be safe and effective to operate. It was an honour just to be asked to do such an important review as it meant that Imperial Oil recognized the skill and expertise of the Big B Engineering Co. as being the best in engineering in order to make any meaningful revisions that would possibly add value to their solid and proven IBPs. Doing this work would also solidify the Big B's reputation as being one of the best engineering firms in the world. It was something definitely worth pursuing.

However, I was not going to do this for another paltry $80,000 fee. The IBPs were far more complex and voluminous and I estimated that it would take at least six weeks to update their specifications and then another six weeks to do the detailed reviews of our revisions and recommendations with Exxon in order for them to agree and accept the changes. Exxon's collective staff of experienced engineers and experts were equal and superior to many of the major engineering design companies in the world. Exxon were so technically strong, they even had their own research and development department. I estimated the engineering fee to be about $300,000 which I relayed to the IOL project manager. He didn't bat an eye at the number and he seemed anxious for us to start as soon as possible.

I said to him, "This amount is a fairly low fee for essentially giving away all our intellectual property and expertise to improve the quality and effectiveness of your specifications. What's in it for us? Why should we want to commit our best people in doing this?" It was a reasonable question since our company would make a lot more money keeping our best people working on the projects we had on hand. "Let me check what IOL is willing to do in this regard," he replied.

The project manager came back with a very unexpected proposal the following day. "If you do this review in the timeframe you outlined, and the results prove to be positive and accepted by Exxon, then how about a $1 million dollars bonus on top of the fee?" Well, that certainly changed the profitability picture and this got the attention of our company. A potential million dollars for essentially doing six weeks of technical work which we were fully capable of doing, and doing well! It was a no-brainer and I was very confident that we could achieve this bonus. We were set to get a formal contract in place and then to proceed with this work immediately.

However, as fate intervened, it was too good to be true. Mike G. was the VP in charge of setting up this contract with IOL. He was advised that although the Big B Engineering Co. and Imperial Oil wanted to sign the contract, this work was not sanctioned nor approved by our respective parent companies Bechtel and Exxon. Apparently, there were some ongoing contractual and legal conflicts between the two major powerhouse companies that were unresolved and they didn't want any new contracts to be made between them that would jeopardize their legal positions while they were still in litigation. As their legal issues involved hundreds of millions of dollars, this possible $1 million bonus was fairly inconsequential to them even though our Canadian office would have benefitted greatly from it. This contractual impasse lasted well over three months, and at the end, the contract was never signed by Imperial. Both IOL and the Big B Engineering Co. were disappointed, but there was nothing they could have done. This opportunity disappeared just as quickly as it had appeared.

As a follow-up to this story, IOL still wanted to have their IBPs reviewed and updated to accommodate the colder winter conditions in Canada. They eventually asked another engineering firm, the Big WP Engineering Co. to do this review. I didn't know whether this company was offered the same $1 million dollars bonus. However, I did get feedback that IOL were not pleased at all with the results and work from the Big WP Engineering and the IBPs were never updated as a consequence.

There is truth in the saying, *"People are not the most important asset. The right people are. And doing the right things with the right people will always produce the right results."* This proved to be so true and the $1 million dollars bonus was not meant to be. I always wondered what could have been. Ah, but that's life when events and windows of opportunity, opening and closing, can be so unpredictable and random.

Chapter 9

LIFE IN RETIREMENT

Story #44

LIFE IN RETIREMENT

If you are nearing or contemplating retirement, let me tell you how difficult it is to adjust to retirement life, especially for men. Sure, people would say, "What's your problem? If I could retire, I would do it right now!" Well, my problem is .... my wife! For some reason no matter how hard I tried, I kept getting in her way. It didn't help when there were just the two of us left in the house after all our children had gone to live their separate lives. My wife had been retired for many years before I did and she was already enjoying her retirement. You could say that I definitely disrupted her daily routines. Not intentionally, I was just being me! She claimed that she was experiencing the Japanese housewives' syndrome when their married–to-work husbands went on mandatory retirement. Married to work? I thought I was married to my wife! Anyway, she found me to be bossy, opinionated, and really unfocused as to what I wanted to do in my retirement. To top it off, I even insisted that she make me a hot lunch every day! And on time! From my perspective, I wasn't being unreasonable in any of my expectations. My wife didn't like it one bit at all. She tried to prepare me (or the better word, to "educate me") on what I needed to do when I retired. The primary requirement for me was to not "get in her way" and not to expect her to be at my beck and call! That was how she felt!

She made me go to a retirement seminar and then read this book, "You Could Live a Long Time. Are You Ready?" by Lyndsay Green. This book had some excellent advice which helped me achieve a better understanding of the perils associated with retirement and how to attain a more harmonious relationship with the one you love.

I have summarized these "Rules for Retirement" in the Appendix. The following are the main points to consider in your retirement:

RULE #1
<u>Confirm Your Mate for Life is Indeed Your Mate for Life</u>

While this seems to be a no brainer, it is the biggest factor in achieving a successful retirement. The consultant at the seminar surprised me by saying that the highest rate of divorce for married couples is in the 50-70 years-old group when most retirements happen. Little idiosyncrasies and annoying habits which we had overlooked or ignored in our partners during our early years of marriage years suddenly became magnified when living together 24/7. I felt this first-hand as my wife and I seemed to have disagreements on almost everything, mostly of the trivial nature. I'm sure that I was bugging her as much as she was bothering me. I couldn't accept the fact that she felt that she was right all the time, even when she was wrong! We would argue about one thing or another every day! It got so bad that it brought me to the brink of the cliff where I felt I was standing at the edge asking myself, "Will I be better off without my wife?" Yes, it was that serious for me. But I think every couple goes through similar conflicts in their relationship. Sometimes, you just need to be pushed to your limit before you recognize the many things you have taken for granted all your life.

Well, I looked out over the cliff and decided not to jump. I rationalized that being with my wife was definitely better than being without her. I confirmed to her that she is indeed my mate for life and that I would try not to annoy her by arguing so much. Actually, what I meant was that I would no longer argue with her even when I know she is wrong. I would just keep my mouth shut and not say anything. If she was wrong, then it would come out eventually. And when that happened, I wouldn't gloat and say "I told you so!" Thank goodness she was still making me a hot lunch every day! In return, I had expected my wife to reciprocate and to confirm to me that I was indeed her mate for life. She remained silent on this matter. When I asked her, all she said was, "You are still on probation!" Women! I can't understand them at all!

RULE #2
<u>Establish Support From Family and Friends</u>

You may not realize this, but we take our family and friends for granted. We expect that they will be there when we need help and that they will do the right things for us and that they will have our best interest at heart. That's a tall order. Everyone will have their own lives to live, their own problems to deal with, and taking care of others can be an imposition and hardship on their own life. So be nice to your family. Reconcile with those you have strained relations with. Make new friends, but more importantly, maintain the goods friends you currently have. I realize that this takes time and a lot of effort to cultivate good friendships. But it is well worth it. Long term friends are like family. I am fortunate that I have two sons who will look after us when my wife and I are no longer able to care for ourselves. Our sons have assured me that when that time comes, they will definitely put me in an excellent nursing home! Well, I expect at least that much! I'm not too sure where my wife will put me since I am still on probation! However, both my wife and I agree that under no circumstances will we ever impose on our sons to live with them and their families when we can no longer care for ourselves.

RULE #3
<u>Make a Work Plan Instead of a Retirement Plan</u>

The retirement consultant said that golfing seven days a week and travelling all over the world may be fine retirement objectives, but they should be only minor parts of your overall plan. Your work plan must include doing things in which you find pleasure on a consistent basis and which will replace whatever satisfaction you got from your previous work life. If you hated what you are doing at work, then retirement will be a snap! Working part time can be part of your work plan if you really like working. Or volunteering, if that is a passion for you. I found writing to be a very satisfying endeavour. Retirement can be a great and stress-free phase in your golden years. You get up when you want, or sleep as late as you want, spend whatever days you choose doing things that you enjoy, like golfing, hiking, shopping and travelling, or doing nothing at all! But be sure that you are financially solid and that you are relatively healthy. Retirement presents opportunities for you to do all the things you couldn't do because you had to work. I also have artistic skills which I have suppressed for years because I found out very early that artists don't make enough money to pay the bills the way engineering could. Some of my friends are still expecting me to paint my series of the "Group of Seven Nudes!" Now, I have no excuse.

RULE #4
<u>Take Care of Yourself – Physically and Mentally</u>

I have a friend who worked very hard all his life and he made a reputation as being the best in his field. But he didn't look after his own health with the same zeal as he did with his career. As a consequence, when he retired, he physically couldn't enjoy the fruits of his life-long labour. How sad. It's true what they say, *"You have nothing unless you have your health."* The quality of life you expect in retirement is directly tied to your physical and mental health. If you have health issues, get them looked after immediately when they occur. Don't procrastinate. Change your diet and exercise regularly to improve your health. Do things which will keep your brain active.

If you have plans to write your memoirs, do it while you can still remember the details of your life and before your memory fades away. Artwork and writing have provided me with the mental stimulation I needed. Continued part-time work is also good if you still enjoy working. I've been practicing my Texas Hold-em techniques for many years now. I plan one day to go to Las Vegas and enter a tournament and win millions! Okay, hundreds will do. My wife thinks that I have just been wasting my time playing games on the computer! But that is the beauty of retirement. It's my time to waste if that is what I want. And I won't be in my wife's way! But for some reason, my wife still wants to influence the things I might want to do in retirement. For example, if I am writing my stories, there better not be a chapter all about her! I don't know how this can be done excluding my mate for life! Even if I am still on probation!

APPENDIX
<u>Rules For Retirement</u>

<u>Author's Note:</u>
The following summary is my own version of "Coles Notes" (I may be dating myself) highlighting the key points of the excellent book on retirement, ***"You Could Live A Long Time. Are You Ready?" by Lyndsay Green.*** I did my best to capture and summarize all the relevant points made by Ms. Green. However, I encourage you to read the actual book for more details and other "gems" of wisdom and knowledge in her book.

<u>Summary Highlights of the Book:</u>

A   <u>The Emotional Circle</u>

1. Confirm that your partner is truly your "partner for life".
2. Keep contact and maintain relationships with current friends. Make new friends.
3. Family members are important for future caring and support. Your children will be choosing your nursing home!
4. Treat your family better. Reconcile with family members.
5. Grandchildren are a great source of joy and purpose for you.

6. Those who do not have family or children will need to rely on very close friends. Make sure you have such friends.

B <u>Self</u>

1. You must be self-aware. You must know who you are and be comfortable in being yourself.
2. Keep your values and integrity. Lead a good life. Share your knowledge and wisdom.
3. Keep your dignity and give up your pride. Learn to ask for and accept help when you need it.
4. Maintain a good sense of humor and never stop laughing. Have a positive attitude. Don't let getting old depress you.
5. Recognize that there will be indignities in aging, but you can also take advantage of being old, eg. senior discounts, not being expected to lift heavy objects and not remembering names!
6. Stay active, but modify your activities to your capabilities as they decline with age. Hitting off the lady's tee in golf will one day be okay!
7. You will regret things that you didn't do, more than the things you did.
8. Plan for the future, but be prepared to go when opportunities arise, eg., especially when friends invite you to join them on a cruise or a golfing trip! Do it while you still can.

9. Be at peace with your spiritual beliefs on the meaning of Life and its purpose *[Tony's]*

C   <u>Civic Engagement</u>

1. If you choose to do volunteer work, make sure it is something you have a passion and desire to do. Once you have decided what you want to do, then don't procrastinate, do it!
2. By giving to others, you will receive. Confucius said: *"I sought for happiness and happiness eluded me. I turned to service and happiness found me."*
3. Volunteering and helping people are good for your soul.

D   <u>Work</u>

1. For many people, continuing to work (either full-time or part-time) is still part of a successful retirement.
2. You need to prepare a Work Plan instead of a Retirement Plan.
3. Decide what you want to do to replace the time you previously spent on work. Take courses, if necessary, to pursue alternate paths: eg., new computer skills, cooking classes, getting ready to enter a Texas Hold-em tournament, writing, painting, investment courses, etc.

4. If you want to continue work, then under what circumstances? What are you looking for in the job? As a mentor or coach? Part-time basis, or work just during the winters only? How much compensation?
5. Has your previous career side-tracked you from doing something else you had always wanted to do in your life? You can do it now!

E   <u>Home</u>

1. Decide what kind of home and where you want to live while you are still able. Plan for the different types of future housing options as you age. Moving will be difficult as you get older.
2. Where you live will determine whether you can live well. Plan for the last one.
3. Start organizing your stuff and prepare to downsize. If you don't control your things, your things will control you. Don't leave this burden for others to take care of because you didn't do it when you had the time and ability to do so. *[Tony's]*

F   <u>Body</u>

1. Recognize that your body will continue to age and deteriorate. That is a fact of life.

2. Take care of your health, by addressing the medical ailments as they occur – body, sight, hearing. Don't wait as they won't get better by doing nothing or ignoring them.

3. Understand what causes your stress and what you need to do to avoid/relieve such conditions.

4. Know your limitations and what your body can do. Hitting a golf ball over 200 yards is quite an achievement for someone over 60 yrs. old. Don't expect to do it all the time!

5. Maintain a healthy lifestyle – eating properly and exercising regularly. Stay in shape – take up walking, biking, golf, pickle ball, yoga, tai chi, dancing, swimming, hiking, shopping, whatever physical activity you can still do and enjoy.

6. Being sexually active is part of this healthy lifestyle. Enjoy it while you can! And when you can't anymore, you will still have many enduring memories!

7. Strive to be happy as happier people tend to be healthier.

G <u>Brain</u>

1. Use it or lose it. Exercise your mind – crossword puzzles, quizzes, memory exercises, writing and reading, playing chess or bridge, watching Jeopardy, etc.

2. Keep your mind engaged and active through work, volunteer activities and hobbies.
3. To stop learning is to start aging. Life is full of wonders that you may have yet to experience.
4. Share your accumulated knowledge, experience and wisdom with others.

H <u>Finances</u>

1. Money matters, but accept that it can't buy everything. Happiness is a frame of mind.
2. Having money means you simply have more choices. But you still have to decide what to do.
3. You don't really need money to be happy. Having more possessions may mean that you just have more stuff to look after. *[Tony's]*
4. As you get older, you actually need less money, unless you have medical problems. Then money does make a difference in the quality of the physical aspects of your remaining life.
5. You will need someone, family or friend, who can be entrusted (power of attorney) to take care of your money and to do what is best for you when you become incapacitated.
6. Plan and settle your funeral arrangements in advance. Don't rely on others to do what you could do yourself. *[Tony's]*

7. If you intend to leave a legacy to family/friends, make and leave a formal will to avoid family disputes and disagreements.
8. Confirm a Personal Directive document detailing such things as organ donations and "Do Not Resuscitate" instructions. *[Tony's]*

I   Legacy

1. If you have grand-children, be part of their lives, influencing them with your values and wealth of knowledge and experience. Help young people to maximize their potential. *[Tony's]*
2. Write your memoirs while you have the mental capacity and energy to do so. Events, people and details will certainly be harder to remember as you get older.
3. Document your family history as a written legacy for your future generations to enjoy. Keep a journal of your important events. Written records last longer than verbal conversations. *[Tony's]*

J   The Future

1. Old people should be treated with reverence and respect for what they have lived through

and experienced in their lives. They still have much to offer. Aging is a gift in Life.

2. Embrace your old age and the experiences associated with growing old. Accept whatever Fate deals you. That is part of Life. *[Tony's]*

3. Accept that Death is our ultimate destination. It is inevitable. This acceptance will free you from un-necessary stress and worry. Look forward to Death when your time comes, and wonder at the possibilities beyond this Life. *[Tony's]*

Chapter 10

THE LAST STORY

Story #45

WHAT'S IN A NAME?

This last story is a very personal one for me and I feel comfortable now in sharing it with you. Please excuse the language used. I could not have written this story without using that word! This story is about my Chinese name.

My English name is Tony Yep. And yes, I do have a Chinese name given to me by my father. It is Yep Fook Hin. The Yep is pronounced like "yip" and it means "leaf" in Chinese. Fook is pronounced like "book", but with the "f" sound instead and "Hin" rhymes with "wean" with the "h" sound. The "Fook" character is a very prestigious and important word in the Chinese culture. This symbol 福 is used everywhere to denote prosperity, happiness and good fortune. Because my father was a farmer back in China, "Hin" means field. Literally translated, Fook Hin means "Bountiful Fields" or "Fields of Plenty". This is a very good name in China.

However, I was never really conscious of what my Chinese name meant to me, nor did I use it while I was growing up. I always used my English name, Tony, and I didn't think about it too much until later in my life. My mother, who only spoke Chinese to me, always called me "Hin", which I accepted as normal, until one eventful day.

It occurred years ago during a car trip I had with my first boss when I had graduated and started to work as an engineer. He was of German descent and he knew little of Chinese customs. We were driving to a jobsite and we got to talking about different nationalities and customs. He asked me whether I had a Chinese name.

"Yes", I said. "It is Fook Hin. It means Bountiful Fields." He glanced at me and I could see some puzzlement in his eyes. "Say that again?"

"Fook Hin", I replied again speaking as phonetically correct in my Chinese dialect as I could.

"What? Say that again!"

"Fook Hin", I repeated loudly, now somewhat irritated that he had such a hard time remembering this name.

"**Fook Hin**!" I said one last time, almost shouting.

He looked over and I could see a twinkle in his eyes as he said to me in a very straight face. "Well, I don't know about you, Tony, *but it sure sounds like a lot of fucking to me!*"

He then turned away, grinning as he continued to drive. I was dumbstruck as I never ever considered my Chinese name in that context. This means that I have been a fucking person all my life?! I was speechless and flabbergasted.

Since that day, I have never purposely told any non-Asian person what my Chinese name was. They simply would not understand and then they would have a hard time trying not to make fun of my name. But now if they asked, I would tell them this story. On the positive side, there was one good thing about all this. I was extremely glad my father didn't name me "Fook Yue" as I would have insulted a lot of people in my life!

So, what's in a name? In my case, it's "Fook Hin" plenty! Please excuse my language! I can't help myself! As I get older and my skin gets thicker and more wrinkled with age, it doesn't matter anymore what people call me as long as they remember me even if it happens to be for my phonetically incorrect Chinese name!

RECOMMENDED READING

Chan Kwok Bun – "Smoke and Fire – The Chinese in Montreal" – 1991 - The Chinese University Press (Hong Kong)

Richard P. Feynman – "Surely You're Joking, Mr. Feynman" – 1985 – Unwin Paperbacks

Lyndsay Green – "You Could Live a Long Time: Are you Ready?" – 2010 – Thomas Allen Publishers

Tony Yep – "Words of Wisdom for Living Life – A Book of Philosophical Thoughts on Life" – 2020 - Amazon-Kindle Direct Publishing (KDP)

Tony Yep – "Quality Management Works!" 1996 Project Management Institute (PMI) Symposium in Calgary. This article is about the differences between a democratic versus an autocratic management style. The concepts are still valid today. Available on the author's website: ***https://drygon.ca***

ABOUT THE AUTHOR

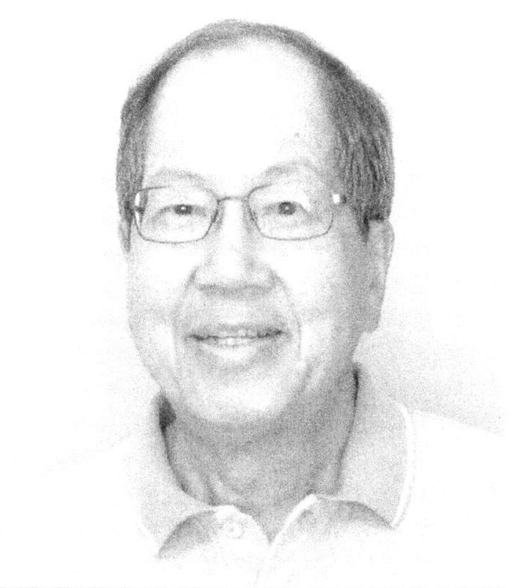

Tony Yep is a Mechanical Engineer by profession, having graduated from McGill University in 1971. He has had a very successful career as an engineering and project manager. Tony has been married for almost 50 years to his soulmate and wife, Patricia. They have two sons, Ted and Tim, and four grandchildren – Kyle, Evan, Gwen and Nathan.

ABOUT THE AUTHOR

In his retirement, he took up writing books as a "second career." In reality, it was something he always wanted to do and writing kept his mind engaged and sharp. His first book, "Words of Wisdom for Living Life – A Book of Philosophical Thoughts on Life" was very serious and thought provoking on the topic of the true meaning of life. This second book is semi-biographical, recounting stories that his father told him and it includes some of his best stories from his personal experiences and insightful observations of people. This book is definitely much easier to read and enjoy.

If you like his books, please let him know by contacting the links below:

<u>Contact Info:</u>

Website: https://drygon.ca
Email: tyep49@gmail.com
Social Media: LinkedIn

Author's Page URL:
Amazon.com/author/tonyyep